The BEAST

That Was, and Is Not, and Yet Is

Melvin Winfrey

Melvin Winfrey

melwinfrey2009@gmail.com

Table of Contents

FOREWORD

I was born in a small town in Louisiana. My father and mother were Baptist. They went to a Baptist church, but they did not learn anything according to the word of God. So I came out of the Baptist church and started to attend different churches. I found one I really liked—a Pentecostal church. I then started to read the Bible carefully. It was then that I realized that these churches, including the Pentecostal churches, were teaching doctrine that wasn't true. I then started to listen to preachers on the radio and continued to read my Bible. I realized the preachers, teachers, and prophets on the radio air were teaching false doctrines, too. All of these were factors led me to write this book. I thought I would be able to help someone to use and understand the Bible. However, with God's help, I hope to deliver the truth to the people. For my help cometh from God.

This book took me years to write. I started out just listening to the radio and the news on television. I then started taking notes and following along in the Bible. Before you know it, I was addicted to reading the Bible. I was more interested than ever before. At first, it was like looking at a bunch of loose pieces to the puzzle, but once I got started, it got easier and easier. I enjoy reading the Bible, and I hope that you are able to follow along and understand it, too. I think God has blessed me with enough wisdom to share and help others learn also. I repeat myself constantly just like the Bible. Constant repetition will help you learn and understand. I hope you enjoy reading this book. May God bless you.

DANIEL 7

In the Bible, Daniel 7:1 reads, "In the first year of Belshazzar king of Babylon, Daniel had a dream and visions of his head upon his bed: then he wrote the dream, and told the sum of the matters."

Now, rightly dividing the word of truth where it says, "Daniel had a dream," we look to Numbers 12:6 and Amos 3:7 for further clarification. Numbers tells a story of a time when Miriam and Aaron spoke against Moses because he married an Ethiopian woman. As punishment, God put upon Miriam leprosy, and she became white as snow. The Lord says, "And he said, Hear now my words: If there be a prophet among you, I the LORD will make myself known unto him in a vision, and will speak unto him in a dream". (Num. 12:6). This is what the Lord did with Daniel. When the Lord speaks, his words are true.

Amos 3:7 offers further enlightenment: "Surely the Lord GOD will do nothing, but he revealeth his secret unto his servants the prophets." This passage is saying that before God does something, he tells his servants—the prophets—before he punishes the people, a nation, or a city. God will tell the prophets because his secret is with the righteous. It is just like in the first Babylon when God sent the prophets Jeremiah and Ezekiel to warn the people what would come to pass if they did not repent, that judgment would come upon them if they did not stop doing evil.

And so it will be at the end time. God will send two witnesses to warn his people to stop sinning. In the New Testament, God sent the prophets by two or three, instead of one like in the Old Testament. Some of the present-day lying prophets and men still believe God sends prophets by one, like he did in the Old Testament, but that is not true. The New Testament, the word of God says, "Let the prophets speak two or three, and let the other judge" (1 Cor. 14:29). Jesus also sent his disciples out by two.

False prophets have spread so many falsehoods that no truth is found in churches anymore. They have the truth mixed up with lies, and they are filled with corruption. The church people have left God. But the truth can be found in the word of God.

Let us turn back to the scriptures, specifically where it says in Daniel 7:1, "visions of his head upon his bed." Further explanation of this phrase can be found in Daniel 2:28: "But there is a God in heaven that revealeth secrets, and maketh known to the king Nebuchadnezzar what shall be in the latter days. Thy dream, and the visions of thy head upon thy bed, are these:" This passage shows that God makes known to his servants, the prophets, "thy dream, and the visions of thy head upon thy bed,"

Now, if we continue to Daniel 7:2, it reads, "Daniel spake and said, I saw in my vision by night, and, behold, the four winds of the heaven strove upon the great sea." The four winds of the heaven means war and the scattering of people. God's people will be scattered in all the nations because they have sinned against God. He will scatter the power of the holy people. The four winds of the heaven are the four great beasts, and these four great beasts will fight upon the earth and make war with the saints. These four beasts, these four kings, will make war with the nations. War causes famines and pestilences and earthquakes. But that's all God's doing because people have sinned against him. People have to be punished because they have not repented.

The four winds are mentioned also in the book of Zechariah: "Ho, ho, come forth, and flee from the land of the north, saith the LORD: for I have spread you abroad as the four winds of the heaven, saith the LORD." (Zech. 2:6). God scatters his people in to all the nations around the world.

The books of Deuteronomy, Ezekiel, and Leviticus also further elaboration on the scattering of people. In Deuteronomy, it reads, "And the LORD shall scatter thee among all people, from the one end of the earth even unto the other; and there thou shalt serve other gods, which neither thou nor thy fathers have known, even wood and stone." (Deut. 28:64). Leviticus 26:33 says, "And I will scatter you among the heathen, and will draw out a sword after you: and your land shall be desolate and your cities waste." In Ezekiel, it reads, "And all his fugitives with all his bands shall fall by the sword, and they that remain shall be scattered toward all winds: and ye shall know that I the LORD have spoken it." (Ezek 17:21). These passages show that God scatters his people because they have sinned against him. This is what is starting to happen today. Wars are starting to occur, and the true Christians shall be persecuted. This is what happened to God's people in the first Babylon.

Now let us return to the book of Daniel. Daniel 7:3 reads, "And four great beast came up from the sea, diverse one from another." The waters represent people in the earth, therefore it means that the four great beasts that "came up from the sea," came out of the earth, from the people. The beasts did not exercise their power at the same time, except the third beast. The third beast had four rulers, four kingdoms. It these kingdoms are China, the bear, the mouth of the lion, and the Vatican—the false prophet. However, the false prophet will pluck up the leopard, the bear, and the lion. I will speak more about the third beast and its four rulers later.

The second part of Daniel's vision—"came up from the sea, diverse one from another."—is also mirrored in book of Revelation. Revelation 13:1 reads, "And I stood upon the sand of the sea, and saw a beast rise up out of the sea, having seven heads and ten horns, and upon his horns ten crowns, and upon his heads the name of the blasphemy." In this passage, John saw a beast rise up out of the sea. The beast he saw encompasses all four beasts in Daniel 7:2–7. The passage also includes the ten horns, the ten kings, and the little horn (the false prophet) that occurs in Daniel, but we will address that later.

Let's move on to Daniel 7:4. It reads, "The first was like a lion, and had eagle's wings; I beheld till the wings thereof were plucked, and it was lifted up from the earth, and made stand upon the feet as a man, and a man's heart was given to it." To further clarify the description of the first beast (a lion with an eagle's wings) and how it applies to events in the modern day, we turn to the books of Deuteronomy, 2 Samuel, Jeremiah, Ezekiel, and Habakkuk. For the rest of the verses not mentioned below, you may read on your own.

Deuteronomy 28:49 reads, "The LORD shall bring a nation against thee from far, from the end of the earth, as swift as the eagle flieth, a nation whose tongue thou shalt not understand;". If we apply this passage to modern day events, we can see that the United States is the eagle, and it came from far to the Iraq people. So these modern day events are God's doing: to punish people for their sins. God said, "And I will punish the world for their evil," and he said "evil shall go forth from nation to nation,"

Second Samuel 1:23 says, "Saul and Jonathan were lovely and pleasant in their lives, and in their death they were not divided: they were swifter than eagles, they were stronger than lions." Like a lion, the United States moves swiftly against other nations, and it always attacks others nations at night. A beast doesn't wait for its enemy or prey to attack before it takes action. A beast will attack first, especially at night: that is why it is called a beast.

Now Jeremiah 4:7 reads, "The lion is come up from his thicket, and the destroyer of the Gentiles is on his way; he is gone forth from his place to make thy land desolate; and thy cities shall be laid waste, without an inhabitant." This passage, too, can be applied to today's events. See how Iraq is being made desolate and the cities laid to waste. There is so much killing, violence, and bloodshed. The seal was opened on September 11, 2001, and the first trumpet sounded when President Bush went to war shortly after the World Trade Center towers fell.

We have hail and fire, mingled with blood, in the land and in the world. When we have stormy weather, we have hail. During summer and fall, we have fire in the land. We have war in the world, and that means bloodshed. The first trumpet has sounded. Bush is the first king. Now Iraq is being made desolate. This is what will happen to many nations and cities. We have four beasts to go through before it will all be over. The last beast will be the worst of them all. The great persecution is coming for the true saints of God.

Now if we return to Daniel 7:4, it says the first beast "was like a lion, and had eagle's wings; I beheld till the wings thereof were plucked,". From this, we can interpret that the United States' horn will be plucked. There will no longer be a super power in the world. Notice where it then says, "and it was lifted up from the earth" (Dan. 7:4). This is comparable to when the United States went to Afghanistan and Iraq: they did not touch the earth because they flew there. Then take notice where the verse then it says, "and made stand upon the feet as a man," When the United States armed forces got to Afghanistan and Iraq, they had to get on the ground and stand upon their feet in order to root out the terrorists and try to keep what they called "peace."

The United States doesn't have a heart after God anymore. They took prayer out of the schools, and they don't want you to talk about God or Jesus Christ in public places. The only thing they talk about is human rights, women's rights, children's rights, animal rights, abortion rights, gay rights, and a right to education. Nothing is mentioned about God's commandments and laws. Not only do they not want you talking about God's commandments and laws, but they fail to mention men's rights. What about that? Oh, they don't want to hear about that. So a man's heart was given to the United States. Americans don't have a heart after God anymore. They have changed God's laws. They have changed the truth of God into a lie.

After the horn of the eagle (the United States) is broken or plucked up, the third beast will show up. Before the third beast come in, the second beast will come in because they will overlap each other. "And behold another beast, a second, like to a bear, and it raised up itself on one side, and it had three ribs in the mouth of it between the teeth of it; and they said thus unto it, Arise, devour much flesh." (Dan. 7:5). Let us look closely at the first part of this verse, where it says, "And behold another beast, a second, like to a bear,". Further clarification regarding this phrase can be found in Daniel 2:39: "And after thee shall arise another kingdom inferior to thee, and another third kingdom of brass, which shall bear rule over all the earth." The second beast is the bear, Russia. But he will be inferior to the first beast. The bear will be lower in space and lower in quality. He will rule a specified area for a period of time.

If we further break down Daniel 7:5, we find that the phrase "it raised up itself on one side," means the second beast, the Russian bear, had one dominion and supreme authority. Russia usually fights another nation alone, without any partners or allies, except for the last battle of Armageddon. The verse then goes on to say, "and it had three ribs in the mouth of it between the teeth of it." The three ribs in the beast's mouth are Ukraine, Georgia, Check and Chechnya, They will fight with Russia to devour much flesh. They told Russia to devour much flesh.

When the wings of the eagle were plucked, his horn was broken. Then four stood up for it, the four kingdoms. Now the four kingdoms make up the third beast (also known as the leopard) and the beast's four heads consist of the bear, the lion, China, and the false prophet (the Vatican). The leopard will rule over all the earth. The third beast had four heads, four rulers, and will rule over the earth. As I said before, the second beast, the bear, is Russia. It had three ribs in the mouth of it between the teeth of it. So it had between the teeth of it probably Georgia, Chechnya, Ukraine. They will fight against the second beast, the bear, to devour much flesh. The second beast had one ruler, one dominion. He will rule only in a specified area, part of the world. The third beast, the leopard had four heads, four rulers, four kingdoms. The leopard will rule over all the earth. Now I hope you understand what I have explained about these four great beasts.

We are currently watching the first and, second beast: the lion and the eagle (the United States). The eagle's wings are going to be plucked. His horn is to be broken. After the United States breaks Iran's horn, then his horn is going to be broken.

The fourth beast will pluck up the first three horns. The first three beasts are the lion, the bear, and China. The false prophet will pluck them up by the roots.

Some people think that Germany is a leopard, but Germany's symbol is not a leopard. The leopard (the third beast) is made up of four heads, the four kingdoms. They are the lion, the bear, China, and the false prophet from the Vatican. The false prophet came out from the leopard because the leopard had four heads, four rulers, four kingdoms. He then subdued those three kings. He plucked them up from the roots.

Some people falsely interpret the coming of the Antichrist in Revelation 13:7. Some people think the war in verse 7 is the work of the Antichrist, but it's not. Notice what it says: "And it was given unto him to make war with the saints, and to, overcome them: and power was given him over all kindreds, and tongues, and nations." This is the work of the third beast in Daniel. The third beast had "four heads; and dominion was given to it" (Dan. 7:6). The third beast makes war with the saints, and one of its heads shall be wounded to death.

We are not yet at the third beast. We are still in the stage of the first and, second beast But after one of the third beast's heads is wounded, its deadly wound shall be healed. Then shall power be given unto him to continue forty and two months, which is equivalent to three and a half years. After that, then the Antichrist will come.

So, the Russian bear will rule a while, and then the third beast—the leopard—will come in and rule over the whole earth. The coming of the third beast is illustrated in Daniel 7:6: "After this, I beheld, and lo another, like a leopard, which had upon the back of it four wings of a fowl: the beast had also four heads; and dominion was given to it." This passage shows the leopard has four heads—four rulers after Russia, four kingdoms that will rule over all the earth. As I have previously mentioned, the four heads will consist of the lion, the bear, China, and the false prophet of the Vatican. The third beast will have four kings ruling the whole earth for a while. Then, out of the four of them, the false prophet will pluck these three up, and he will exercise all their power. The false prophet will also have the ten kings with him.

Now, let's return to the Daniel 7:6 and his description of the third beast, specifically where it says, "four heads; and dominion was given to it." To help us better understand the meaning of this passage, we will turn to Daniel 8:8 and 8:22.

Daniel 8:8 says, "Therefore, the he-goat waxed very great: and when he was strong, the great horn was broken; and for it, came up four notable ones toward the four winds of heaven." Let's break this verse down. Where it says, "Therefore, the he-goat waxed very great: and when he was strong, the great horn was broken;" we can interpret that he goat is the United States. His horn is going to be broken, his power in the world. Now continue to where it reads, "and for it, came up four notable ones toward the four winds of heaven." This portion of the verse references the third beast, which will have four notable kings, four notable kingdoms. Where it says, "toward the four winds of heaven." it simply means that the four kings of the third beast shall bear rule over all the earth. These four kings are also the four beasts that appear in Revelation 13:1, which we will talk more about later.

Now let's read Daniel 8:22: "Now that being broken, whereas four stood up for it, four kingdoms shall stand up out of the nation, but not in his power." This means that after the United States' horn (power) is broken, four will stand up and their power will be not of the United State. This further illustrates that the second beast (Russia) will rule a while, and the third beast (the leopard) will then rule for a while.

Now I heard a present-day false prophet say that when the United States' horn is broken, the Antichrist will come. That claim is not true, though he will show up eventually. The truth is that the four kings will show up after the horn is broken. If you read God's word, you will find out the truth for yourself and stop believing everything the false prophets tell you.

Daniel 8:23 reads, "And in the latter time of their kingdom, when the transgressors are come to the full, a king of fierce countenance, and understanding dark sentences, shall stand up." Now where the Bible says, "And in the latter time of their kingdom, when the transgressors are come to the full," it means the third beast (with its four kingdoms)—not the Antichrist —will rule for a while. The Antichrist will show up after the coming of the third beast.

The book Daniel does, however, tell of the coming of the Antichrist. Daniel 7:7,8 reads, "After this I saw in the night visions, and behold a fourth beast, dreadful and terrible, and strong exceedingly; and it had great iron teeth: it devoured and brake in pieces, and stamped the residue with the feet of it: and it was diverse from all the beasts that were before it; and it had ten horns." Now this fourth beast is the false prophet alone with the ten kings. The false prophet is the Antichrist.

Now let's look in detail at where it says, "a fourth beast, dreadful and terrible, and strong exceedingly; and it had great iron teeth:" Additional verses within the book of Daniel provide further clarification. Daniel 2:40 reads, "And the fourth kingdom shall be strong as iron: forasmuch as iron breaketh in pieces and subdueth all things: and as iron that breaketh all these, shall it break in pieces and bruise." This confirms that the fourth beast will be extremely strong.

Daniel 7:19 says, "Then I would know the truth of the fourth beast, which was diverse from all the others, exceeding dreadful, whose teeth were of iron, and his nails of brass; which devoured, brake in pieces, and stamped the residue with his feet;". We can see from this passage that the fourth beast will be different from the other beasts. He will be exceedingly dreadful. Then Daniel 7:23 reads, "Thus he said, The fourth beast shall be the fourth kingdom upon earth, which shall be diverse from all kingdoms, and shall devour the whole earth, and shall tread it down, and break it in pieces." From this passage, we see that the fourth beast will be the fourth kingdom upon earth in the last days.

Now, let's return once again to Daniel 7:7, specifically where it says "and it had ten horns." We can find further clarification on the fourth beast's ten horns both within the book of Daniel and in the book of Revelation. Daniel 2:41 reads, "And whereas thou sawest the feet and toes, part of potters' clay, and part of iron, the kingdom shall be divided; but there shall be in it of the strength of the iron, forasmuch as thou sawest the iron mixed with miry clay." The feet mentioned in this passage, upon which there are a total of ten toes, are the ten horns referred to in Daniel 7:7. Now in the kingdom mentioned in the passage above, the false churches will be mixed in with the government (the iron and the false churches). The people (the saints) will be persecuted in the real church.

Now we will move to Revelation 13:1 where it says, "And I stood upon the sand of the sea, and saw a beast rise up out of the sea, having seven heads and ten horns, and upon his horns ten crowns, and upon his heads the name of blasphemy." This also is a reference to the fourth beast with its ten crowned horns—the ten kings. The ten kings will come before the Antichrist takes power.

The first king before these ten will be the lion with eagle's wings. Looking at these kings in today's context, this first king is Britain and the United States. We are currently watching the first and second beast Now after the U.S horn is plucked, we will have two more beast rulers to come.

Daniel 7:8 continues to tell about the coming of the Antichrist: "And I considered the horns, and behold there came up among them another little horn, before whom there were three of the first horns plucked up by the roots: and behold, in the horn were eyes like the eyes of man, and a mouth speaking great things." The ten horns (the ten kings) came up first, and then the little horn came up among them. Then the little horn will pluck up the first three horns by the roots. So out of all of these beasts that shall rule, there will be a total seven kings, as illustrated in Revelation 13.1.

Now in Daniel 8:8, it reads, "Therefore, the he-goat waxed very great: and when he was strong, the great horn was broken; and for it came up four notable ones toward the four winds of heaven." This further illustrates that when the horn of the United States (the first beast) is broken, plucked up, four will stand up for its power. The Antichrist will come out of these four, and he will pluck up the other three beasts—the lion, the bear, and—China

Now go back to Daniel 7:8 to where it says, "there came up among them another little horn, before whom there were three of the first horns plucked up by the roots:" Further clarification on this passage can be found in verses 20, 21, and 24 of the seventh chapter of the book of Daniel. Now you will see, ten horns came first and then the little horn (the Antichrist) came up among them. Then he plucked up the first three horns.

Now Daniel 7:20 says, "And of the ten horns that were in his head, and of the other which came up, and before whom three fell; even of that horn that had eyes, and a mouth that spake very great things, whose look was more stout than his fellows." This means that the ten horns came up first before the Antichrist. The false prophet came up among these ten horns, the ten kings. Then the false prophet subdued the first three kings who he was within the third beast The Antichrist is the false prophet, and he was stouter, stronger, braver, and more powerful than his fellows.

Next, Daniel 7:21 reads, "I beheld, and the same horn made war with the saints, and prevailed against them;". The little horn, the false prophet, will make war with the saints and not with animals. Now some of the false prophets and men of today's churches say that when the Jews go back to performing animal sacrifices, that will make the abomination that maketh desolate, but that is not true. That Antichrist will set up an image, like Nebuchadnezzar did in the first Babylon, and he will want everybody to bow down to it. That will make the abomination that maketh desolate.

Now Daniel 7:24 reads, "And the ten horns out of this kingdom are ten kings, that shall arise: and another shall rise after them; and he shall be diverse from the first, and he shall subdue three kings." This further illustrates that the Antichrist will rise after the ten horns.

Some of the false prophets of today are trying to claim that the little horn is the United States, but that is not true. The United States and Britain are the first beast. The little horn is the last beast, the fourth beast (the false prophet). Many people don't have the wisdom and knowledge to understand this. Others simply cannot think for themselves.

The Bible also talks about the ten kings in Revelation 17:12. It says, "And the ten horns which thou sawest are ten kings, which have received no kingdom as yet; but receive power as kings one hour with the beast." This passage shows that these ten kings receive power as kings for one hour with the false prophet, the Antichrist.

Most people have a hard time understanding Revelation 17:10–11. In verse 10 it says, "And there are seven kings: five are fallen, and one is, and the other is not yet come; and when he cometh, he must continue a short space." There are seven kings that will rule upon the earth in these four kingdoms, four beasts upon earth. Let me now explain the seven kings.

The first king was like a lion and had eagle's wings. This is the United States and Britain. The United States came out from Britain.

They are allies. The United States is the head spokesman. The second beast is like a bear, which is Russia. That is the second king. The third beast is like a leopard, and that beast had also four heads. It had four rulers, which are four more kings. Now out of those four kings are the leopard China the bear (Russia), the mouth of the lion (Britain), and the Vatican or false prophet (the pope of Rome). The United States and Britain work together as allies. Britain's symbol is two lions facing each other. The United States' symbol is an eagle. That makes a total of six kings. Now, the ten horns shall arise (the ten kings), which is the fourth beast. The fourth beast shall be the fourth kingdom upon the earth. The fourth beast shall be the seventh king. Then the false prophet, the Antichrist shall arise among them, and he will pluck up the first three kings that were with him (the lion, the bear, and China).

So, though the little horn technically makes the eighth king, he is actually included in the seven because he joined in with the ten kings. The ten kings receive power as kings one hour with the beast.

Now Revelation 17:11 reads, "And the beast that was, and is not, even he is the eighth, and is of the seven, and goeth into perdition." It says, "the beast that was, and is not." He was part of the third beast because the third beast had four heads. The little horn came out from the third beast, and he had the ten kings with him, which made him the fourth beast. He plucked up the three other heads of the third beast. So the fourth beast is "the beast that was, and is not, and yet is." (Rev. 17:8). He was part of the third beast—the leopard. As I mentioned previously, the leopard had four heads: heads of the lion, the bear, China, and the Vatican (also known as the false prophet or the Pope).

Now I hope you understand what I have explained. Allow me to reiterate the formulation of the seven kings: The first beast, the first king, is the United States (George Bush). The second is the bear, Russia. That equals two kings. The third beast had four heads, so there were four kings in the third beast (the lion, the bear, and China, and the false prophet). That equals six kings. So now the fourth beast will have ten kings, but their power will equal one. That makes seven kings. Then little horn will come up among them, making the eighth king, but he is also of the seven because he will join in with the ten kings. So the little horn, the false prophet, is the eighth king, but is of the seven. So that means the eighth is also of the seven.

Now Daniel 7:9 reads, "I beheld till the thrones were cast down, and the Ancient of days did sit, whose garment was white as snow, and the hair of his head like the pure wool: his throne was like the fiery flame, and his wheels as burning fire." This passage means that after the coming of the Antichrist (the fourth beast), Jesus Christ will return.

Now rightly dividing the word of truth in verse 9 where it says, "I beheld till the thrones were cast down," we turn again to the book Revelation for further clarification. Revelation 20:4 reads, "And I saw thrones, and they sat upon them, and judgment was given unto them: and I saw the souls of them that were beheaded for the witness of Jesus, and for the word of God, and which had not worshipped the beast, neither his image, neither had received his mark upon their foreheads, or in their hands; and they lived and reigned with Christ a thousand years." This passage shows that the Antichrist, his government, and his thrones were cast down. The saints sat upon the thrones and judgment was given unto them. This means the saints of the most high will take the kingdom.

Further clarification of the passage, "the Ancient of days did sit," (Daniel 7:9) can be found in Psalm 90:2 and Daniel 7:13 and 7:22. Psalms 90:2 reads, "Before the mountains were brought forth, or ever thou hadst formed the earth and the world, even from everlasting to everlasting, thou art God." We can see from this passage that God Almighty is the Ancient of days and Jesus Christ.

Now we look to where Daniel 7:13 says, "I saw in the night visions, and, behold, one like the Son of man came with the clouds of heaven, and came to the Ancient of days, and they brought him near before him." This passages shows that Jesus Christ is the first and the last. Then Daniel 7:22 reads, "Until the Ancient of days came, and judgment was given to the saints of the most High; and the time came that the saints possessed the kingdom." The phrase "the Ancient of the days came," means the time when Jesus Christ set up his kingdom here on earth. When that happens, the saints shall rule and reign with Christ for a thousand years.

Now let's return to Daniel 7:9 and explore the remainder of the verse. If we take the next portion, "whose garment was white as snow, and the hair of his head like the pure wool:" we can go to Psalms 104:2 and Revelation 1:14 to help us interpret its meaning. Psalms 104:2 reads, "Who coverest thyself with light as with a garment: who stretchest out the heavens like a curtain:" This verse refers to how the Lord covered himself with light as with a garment Revelation 1:14 reads, "His head and his hairs were white like wool, as white as snow; and his eyes were as a flame of fire;" This verse shows that God is light. Jesus Christ is light. He is not darkness; he is the light. Ungodly people love darkness.

Then, returning once again to Daniel 7:9 where it reads, "and his wheels as burning fire." we can find further clarification in the book of Ezekiel. Ezekiel 1:15 reads, "Now as I beheld the living creatures, behold one wheel upon the earth by the living creatures, with his four faces." This verse is saying God is among the living creatures. Ezekiel 1:16 then reads, "The appearance of the wheels and their work was like unto the color of a beryl: and they four had one likeness: and their appearance and their work was as it were a wheel in the middle of a wheel." This is God's throne. The four living creatures are the same four beasts in Revelation. In these passages, God showed Ezekiel a vision about what was going to happen here on Earth, just as in Revelation when God showed John what was going to happen here on Earth at the end time.

Now, if we continue with Daniel 7:10, it reads, "A fiery stream issued and came forth from before him: thousand thousands ministered unto him, and ten thousand times ten thousand stood before him: the judgment was set, and the books were opened." After the Antichrist and his army are destroyed, the judgment will be set. The saints will sit on the thrones to judge the ungodly people. This will happen immediately after the tribulation of those days.

Let's break that passage down, focusing first on where it says, "A fiery stream issued and came forth from before him:". We can turn to Psalms 50 and 97 and the book of Isaiah to help us interpret deeper meaning.

In Psalm 50, I will read verses 3, 4, and 5 so you can understand. In verse 3 it reads, "Our God shall come, and shall not keep silence: a fire shall devour before him, and it shall be very tempestuous round about him." Note that it will be very stormy around him. Verse 4 says, "He shall call to the heavens from above, and to the earth, that he may judge his people." This means God will judge his people immediately after the great tribulation. The saints shall sit on the thrones and judge the people. Then, verse 5 reads, "Gather my saints together unto me; those that have made a covenant with me by sacrifice." These events will happen after the great tribulation. Additional clarification of Psalm 50:5 can be found in Matthew 24:31, where it says, "And he shall send his angels with a great sound of a trumpet, and they shall gather together his elect from the four winds, from one end of heaven to the other."

Now let's move on to Psalm 97:3: "A fire goeth before him, and burneth up his enemies round about." This is simply stating that the Lord is coming, and he will burn up his enemies. "In flaming fire taking vengeance on them that know not God, and that obey not the gospel of our Lord Jesus Christ:" (2 Thess. 1:8).

Now we turn to the book of Isaiah. Isaiah 30:33 reads, "For Tophet is ordained of old; yea, for the king it is prepared; he hath made it deep and large: the pile thereof is fire and much wood; the breath of the LORD, like a stream of brimstone, doth kindle it." This verse tells us that the breath of the Lord is like a breath of brimstone. Isaiah 66:15 then says, "For, behold, the LORD will come with fire, and with his chariots like a whirlwind, to render his anger with fury, and his rebuke with flames of fire." This passage shows us that the Lord is going to come with flames of fire.

Now let's continue to interpret Daniel 7:10. To gain further insight into the phrase "thousand thousands ministered unto him, and ten thousand times ten thousand stood before him:" (Dan. 7:10), we turn to 1 Kings, Psalms 68, Hebrew, and Revelation.

First Kings 22:19 reads, "And he said, Hear thou therefore the word of the LORD: I saw the LORD sitting on his throne, and all the host of heaven standing by him on his right hand and on his left."

The host of heaven that stand beside him are the angels of God. They will be with the Lord Jesus Christ.

Now Psalm 68:17 reads, "The chariots of God are twenty thousand, even thousands of angels: the Lord is among them, as in Sinai, in the holy place." This passage shows that the Lord will be among the saints, and he is among the saints. Next, let us read Hebrew 12:22: "But ye are come unto mount Zion, and unto the city of the living God, the heavenly Jerusalem, and to an innumerable company of angels,". This verse shows the saints will come as angels. Angels are called saints, too. Finally, Revelation 5:11 reads, "And I beheld, and I heard the voice of many angels round about the throne, and the beasts, and the elders: and the number of them was ten thousand times ten thousand, and thousands of thousands;". This means that the saints and the angels were all one in Christ.

Now we will finish interpreting the last part of Daniel 7:10 where it says, "the judgment was set, and the books were opened." We will look to the book of Revelation for additional insight. Revelation 20:4 reads, "And I saw thrones, and they sat upon them, and judgment was given unto them: and I saw the souls of them that were beheaded for the witness of Jesus, and for the word of God, and which had not worshipped the beast, neither his image, neither had received his mark upon their foreheads, or in their hands; and they lived and reigned with Christ a thousand years." Judgment is given unto the saints. The saints will judge the unrighteous, the wicked. This is why it is important for you to know the law of God. If you don't know God's laws, you won't know when you do wrong.

Revelation 20:12 reads, "And I saw the dead, small and great, stand before God; and the books were opened: and another book was opened, which is the book of life: and the dead were judged out of those things which were written in the books, according to their works." The saints will judge the people who are written about in the books. The wicked and ungodly people will be judged out of the books.

Daniel 7:11 reads, "I beheld then because of the voice of the great words which the horn spake: I beheld even till the beast was slain, and his body destroyed, and given to the burning flame." The beast in this passage is the fourth beast with ten horns, ten kings. It shows that the beast will be destroyed and the people deceived by the false prophet, the ones who had received the mark of the beast and worshiped his image, will be cast into the lake of fire. The false prophet will deceive the whole world except for the very elect.

The church people of today who speak in tongues claim they are Christians who are sanctified and filled with the Holy Ghost. But they are not speaking in tongue. They are speaking in a language they made up. They don't know themselves what they are saying.

Now Daniel 7:12 says, "As concerning the rest of the beasts, they had their dominion taken away: yet their lives were prolonged for a season and time." This passage could possibly be speaking of the first three beasts (three kings) that were plucked up and subdued by the Antichrist, also known as the false prophet. Their lives were prolonged for a season and time.

Next, Daniel 7:13 reads, "I saw in the night visions, and behold, one like the Son of man came with the clouds of heaven, and came to the Ancient of days, and they brought him near before him." The Son of man is Jesus Christ, and he will come back with the clouds of heaven. He will come back the same way he left—with the clouds of heaven. Additional clarification on this verse can be found in Acts chapter 1:9, which reads, "And when he had spoken these things, while they beheld, he was taken up; and a cloud received him out of their sight." The portion of this verse that says "he was taken up; and a cloud received him out of their sight." means he will come back with the clouds of heaven. Immediately after the great tribulation, the Lord will come back.

Now rightly dividing the word of truth in Daniel 7:13 where it says, "one like the son of man came with the clouds of heaven," we turn to the books of Ezekiel, Matthew, and Revelation to learn more. Ezekiel 1:26 reads, "And above the firmament that was over their heads was the likeness of a throne, as the appearance of a sapphire stone: and upon the likeness of the throne was the likeness as the appearance of a man above upon it." In this passage, Jesus Christ was upon the throne with great glory.

Matthew 24:30 says, "And then shall appear the sign of the Son of man in heaven: and then shall all the tribes of the earth mourn, and they shall see the Son of man coming in the clouds of heaven with power and great glory." This further illustrates that the Lord Jesus Christ will come back in the clouds of heaven with power and great glory.

Next, let's look back at Daniel 7:13 where it says, "the Ancient of days, and they brought him near before him." If we turn back to Daniel 7:9, it reads: "I beheld till the thrones were cast down, and the Ancient of days did sit, whose garment was white as snow, and the hair of his head like the pure wool: his throne was like the fiery flame, and his wheels as burning fire." That is when Jesus Christ will come back with the saints, and they will live and reign with Christ for a thousand years.

Moving on to Daniel 7:14, the verse reads, "And there was given him dominion, and glory, and a kingdom, that all people, nations, and languages, should serve him: his dominion is an everlasting dominion, which shall not pass away, and his kingdom, that which shall not be destroyed." This means that all power in heaven and in earth was given unto Jesus Christ, and that all people, nations, and languages, should serve him;

Now let's look at the first part of Daniel 7:14 more closely. The passage that says, "And there was given him dominion, and glory, and a kingdom," can be further interpreted through Psalm 2:6–8; Psalm 8:6; Psalm 110:1–2; Matthew 11:27 and 28:18; John 3:35; 1 Corinthians 15:27; and Ephesians 1:22. For all the verses not mentioned below, you can read on your own.

Psalms 2:6 reads, "Yet have I set my King upon my holy hill of Zion." This means Jesus Christ will rule in Jerusalem. Verse 7 then reads, "I will declare the decree: The Lord hath said unto me, Thou art my Son; this day have I begotten thee." The son is Jesus Christ. Next, verse 8 says, "Ask of me, and I shall give thee the heathen for thine inheritance, and the uttermost parts of the earth for thy possession." This further illustrates that the Lord will rule over all the nations.

Now, returning to the book of Daniel, Daniel 7:15 reads, "I Daniel was grieved in my spirit in the midst of my body, and the visions of my head troubled me." This means Daniel was troubled by what he saw in the visions about the four beasts. His trouble is further illustrated in Daniel 7:28, where it reads, "Hitherto is the end of the matter. As for me Daniel, my cogitations much troubled me, and my countenance changed in me: but I kept the matter in my heart." Daniel was troubled about the fourth beast, which will be the worst time since there was a nation.

Next, Daniel 7:16 reads, "I came near unto one of them that stood by, and asked him the truth of all this. So he told me, and made me know the interpretation of the things." Daniel wanted to know the truth about the interpretations of his visions.

Moving on to Daniel 7:17, it continues, "These great beasts, which are four, are four kings, which shall arise out of the earth." This corresponds with Daniel 7:3 when "four great beasts came up from the sea, diverse one from another." The four kings will arise out of the earth, and they will be different from one another. They will operate their governments separately from each other. As I said earlier, we are currently watching the first and second beast, which is the lion (Britain) and the eagle (United States). The United States will be plucked up. He will have no more power or leadership in the world. Russia will be the second beast. So after the United States, we still have two more beasts to come before Jesus Christ will come back.

Daniel 7:18 continues, "But the saints of the most High shall take the kingdom, and possess the kingdom for ever, even for ever and ever." This means that the kingdom will be given to the saints of the most High. Now divining the word of truth, we find further clarification in Isaiah 60:12–14; Daniel 7:22 and 7:27; 2 Timothy 2:11–12; Revelation 2:26–27, 3:21, and 20:4. For all the verses not listed below, you can read on your own.

Isaiah 60:12 reads, "For the nation and kingdom that will not serve thee shall perish; yea, those nations shall be utterly wasted." This means that those nations shall serve the Lord Jesus Christ and the saints will rule and reign with him. Isaiah 60:13 continues, "The glory of Lebanon shall come unto thee, the fir tree, the pine tree, and the box together, to beautify the place of my sanctuary; and I will make the place of my feet glorious." This says the earth will be beautiful. Then Isaiah 60:14 reads, "The sons also of them that afflicted thee shall come bending unto thee; and all they that despised thee shall bow themselves down at the soles of thy feet; and they shall call thee, The city of the LORD, The Zion of the Holy One of Israel." The people that are left here on Earth in the flesh after the great tribulation will bow themselves down to Jesus. This will take place after the great tribulation, during the thousand-year reign, and after

Daniel 7:22 offers further clarification: "Until the Ancient of days came, and judgment was given to the saints of the most High; and the time came that the saints possessed the kingdom." It means the saints will live here on earth forever and ever.

Daniel 7:27 reads, "And the kingdom and dominion, and the greatness of the kingdom under the whole heaven, shall be given to the people of the saints of the most High, whose kingdom is an everlasting kingdom, and all dominions shall serve and obey him." This means after the false prophet and the ten-horned beast are destroyed, the kingdom will be given to the people of the saints of the most High, and they will take the kingdom forever and ever.

Let's read one more verse regarding the saints' reign: 2 Timothy 2:11–12. Verse 11 reads, "It is a faithful saying: For if we be dead with him, we shall also live with him:" It means that the saints who died with him shall also live with him and reign with him. Next, verse 12 reads, "If we suffer, we shall also reign with him: if we deny him, he also will deny us:" which means we have to suffer in order to reign with him. Only through much tribulation will we enter into his kingdom.

Now we return to the book of Daniel. Daniel 7:19 reads, "Then I would know the truth of the fourth beast, which was diverse from all the others, exceeding dreadful, whose teeth were of iron, and his nails of brass; which devoured, brake in pieces, and stamped the residue with his feet;" Daniel says the Antichrist, false prophet, will stamp the residue with his feet. "Stamp" means to pound, strike, or beat with the foot. This passage means he will try to get rid of the remaining saints that are still living during his reign.

Continuing on, Daniel 7:20 reads, "And of the ten horns that were in his head, and of the other which came up, and before whom three fell; even of that horn that had eyes, and a mouth that spake very great things, whose look was more stout than his fellows."

Remember, the fourth beast had ten horns, ten kings. The ten horns came up first, and then the little horn came up among the ten horns. The little horn plucked up the first three beasts (the lion, the bear, and China). The little horn was stronger, braver, bolder, and more powerful than his fellows.

Then Daniel 7:21 says, "I beheld, and the same horn made war with the saints, and prevailed against them;" The fourth beast, the Antichrist (false prophet) made war with the saints and not with animals. The false prophet will make war with the saints of God. Now in verse 21 where it says, "and the same horn made war with the saints, and prevailed against them;" we can read more about how the Antichrist made war with the saints in Daniel 8:12, 8:24, and 11:31 and Revelation 11:7, 17:14, and 19:19.

Some of the false prophets, teachers, and preachers think these verses in chapter eight of the book of Daniel talk about animal sacrifices, but that is not true. Daniel's prophecy was for the end time. Under the new covenant, the New Testament, the saints are the daily sacrifice. There are no more animal sacrifices in the New Testament. The Antichrist, false prophet, will make war with the saints.

Now let's move on to Daniel 8:12 and 8:24. Verse 12 reads, "And an host was given him against the daily sacrifice by reason of transgression, and it cast down the truth to the ground; and it practiced, and prospered." An army was given to the Antichrist against the saints. The daily sacrifice is the sacrifice of the saints of God under the new covenant in the New Testament. The Antichrist will make war with the saints, some of which will be killed or put into prisons. All the saints will be tried as by fire.

Now Daniel 8:24 reads, "And his power shall be mighty, but not by his own power: and he shall destroy wonderfully, and shall prosper, and practice, and shall destroy the mighty and the holy people." The Antichrist's power shall be mighty, but it will not be by his own power. His power will come from the ten horns: the ten kings. That is how his power will be mighty. He will destroy the mighty and holy people—the saints of God.

Daniel 11:31 tells more about the Antichrists war against the saints. It reads, "And arms shall stand on his part, and they shall pollute the sanctuary of strength, and shall take away the daily sacrifice, and they shall place the abomination that maketh desolate." The phrase "and arms shall stand on his part," means an army will stand on the Antichrist's part, and they will pollute the sanctuary of strength in Jerusalem. Where the verse reads, "and shall take away the daily sacrifice," means they will take away the saints. That will be the time when I believe they will kill the two witnesses and some of the saints. Jerusalem shall be trodden down of the Gentiles. Jerusalem will go into captivity into all nations for three and a half years.

You see, when the Antichrist's army kills the two witnesses, they will set up the abomination that maketh desolate. That is when they will set up an image, and Jerusalem will go into captivity into all the nations. That is when "Jerusalem shall be trodden down of the Gentiles, until the times of the Gentiles be fulfilled." (Luke 21:24). Then, after three and a half years, Jesus Christ will return.

Even more information about the Antichrist's war on the saints can be found in the book of Revelation. Revelation 11:7 reads, "And when they shall have finished their testimony, the beast that ascendeth out of the bottomless pit shall make war against them, and shall overcome them, and kill them." Now you see, this passage further illustrates that the fourth beast in the book of Daniel—the second beast in the book of Revelation—will kill the two witnesses. That is when Jerusalem will go into captivity for three and a half years.

After the beast kills the two witnesses, it will set up an image, and that will be the abomination that maketh desolate. That is the start of the great tribulation, when Jerusalem will go into captivity for three and a half years. The Antichrist will take away the daily sacrifice, the saints, and make war with them.

Now we look to Revelation 13:7. It reads, "And it was given unto him to make war with the saints, and to overcome them: and power was given him over all kindreds, and tongues, and nations." This passage refers to the third beast in the book of Daniel, which was given unto the Antichrist to make war with the saints and to overcome them. The false prophet was among the four heads of the third beast. The third beast made war with the saints and the fourth beast. Remember in Matthew 24:9, before the abomination was set up, these beasts made war with the saints. Its in Mark 13:9, Luke 21:12, and Revelation 13:7. These beasts made war with the saints and the false prophet came up in Revelation 13:11.

Next, Revelation 17:14 reads, "These shall make war with the Lamb, and the Lamb shall overcome them; for he is Lord of lords, and King of kings; and they that are with him are called, and chosen, and faithful." The ten kings of the fourth beast in DANIEL shall make war with the Lord Jesus Christ, which means they will also make war with the saints. The saints will be with the Lord Jesus Christ because they are called the chosen and faithful. The saints will have great persecution and will be in the great tribulation. They will be hated of all nations and all men for the sake of Jesus' name.

It is starting to happen today. The world is filled with violence, and women want to be in control. The women want to be the head over men. Men don't know God anymore. Men don't want to retain any knowledge about God. Men are in a rage because women are ruling over them. This concept will be discussed in more detail a little later.

Let us continue to explore the war on the saints. Revelation 19:19 reads, "And I saw the beast, and the kings of the earth, and their armies, gathered together to make war against him that sat on the horse, and against his army." This shows again that the beast and the kings of the earth will make war against the saints. Remember the Lord said the faithful will be hated by all nations and all men.

It is starting to happen even today. There is no justice in the land. Sin is rapidly increasing, and violence is everywhere. The world is filled with violence and corruption, and we have homosexual people and women running the country. All of these things are ungodly. Men want to be women. The men in the United States will not stand up for righteousness and for justice. Men have become wicked and ungodly. They fail to mention God anymore. The only things men talk about these days are foolishness, sex, and sports. They talk about the love of pleasure rather than the love of God. We are living in the end time, my friends. We are living in a wicked and violent world. We must prepare to meet the Lord right now. Now is the time. We are living in a sad time, a time of sorrow.

Now, returning to the book of Daniel, Daniel 7:22 reads, "Until the Ancient of days came, and judgment was given to the saints of the most High; and the time came that the saints possessed the kingdom." This simply refers to that the beginning of the days when Jesus Christ will rule here on Earth and the saints will be with Him. If we focus on the phrase, "Until the Ancient of days came," we can connect it back to Daniel 7:9, where it reads, "I beheld till the thrones were cast down, and the Ancient of days did sit, whose garment was white as snow, and the hair of his head like the pure wool: his throne was like the fiery flame, and his wheels as burning fire." This passage shows that Ancient of days will sit after the fourth beast, the Antichrist, is destroyed.

Now, Daniel 7:23 reads, "Thus he said, The fourth beast shall be the fourth kingdom upon earth, which shall be diverse from all kingdoms, and shall devour the whole earth, and shall tread it down, and break it in pieces." The fourth beast shall be strong and dreadful. We can interpret further meaning of the phrase "the fourth kingdom upon earth" by referencing Daniel 2:40. It reads, "And the fourth kingdom shall be strong as iron: forasmuch as iron breaketh in pieces and subdueth all things: and as iron that breaketh all these, shall it break in pieces and bruise." That fourth beast (the Antichrist) shall be strong as iron. He will stamp the residue with the feet of it, and cause some of the people to receive the mark of the beast in order to buy or sell.

Next, Daniel 7:24 reads, "And the ten horns out of this kingdom are ten kings, that shall arise: and another shall rise after them; and he shall be diverse from the first, and he shall subdue three kings." As I have already mentioned earlier, the ten kings came up first and then the little horn came up among the ten kings. The little horn plucked up the first three kings.

A lot of these false prophets believe that the end is here today, but that is not true. The end is not here yet. We are just in the beginning of sorrows. Jesus says in Luke 21:9, "But when ye shall hear of wars, and commotions, be not terrified: for these things must first come to pass: but the end is not by and by." The end has not yet come. When you hear of the wars and rumors of wars, the end is not yet here. We are still in the first and second beast We have two more beasts to go through before it will all be over.

Now, returning to Daniel 7:24, let's take a closer look at where it says, "And the ten horns out of this kingdom are ten kings, that shall arise: and another shall rise after them;" This verse references back to Daniel 7:7–8 and 7:20 and Revelation 17:12.

Daniel 7:7 reads, "After this I saw in the night visions, and behold a fourth beast, dreadful and terrible, and strong exceedingly; and it had great iron teeth: it devoured and brake in pieces, and stamped the residue with the feet of it: and it was diverse from all the beasts that were before it; and it had ten horns." Now you see the ten horns, the ten kings, came up first. The little horn showed up after the ten kings.

Now Daniel 7:8 reads, "I considered the horns, and behold, there came up among them another little horn, before whom there were three of the first horns plucked up by the roots: and behold, in this horn were eyes like the eyes of man, and a mouth speaking great things." The Antichrist came up among the ten horns. The false prophet is the Antichrist. And he shall speak great words against the most High against God, and he shall deceive the whole world except the very elect.

Daniel 7:20 further expands upon this concept: "And of the ten horns that were in his head, and of the other which came up, and before whom three fell; even of that horn that had eyes, and a mouth that spake very great things, whose look was more stout than his fellows." You see, the ten horns came up first and the little horn came up among them. That little horn plucked the third beast up. The third beast, which is the leopard, had four heads, which were the four kings. The little horn was among those four, and then the ten kings came up. So the little horn joined with the ten horns, and he came up among them and plucked up the first three beasts (the first three kings by the roots. Now, the little horn looked stouter than his fellows, which means he was stronger, braver, and more powerful than them.

Revelation 17:12 reads, "And the ten horns which thou sawest are ten kings, which have received no kingdom as yet; but receive power as kings one hour with the beast." These ten kings will receive power as kings one hour with the beast.

Now the second beast in Revelation 13:11 "had two horns like a lamb, and he spake as a dragon." That means that the second beast had two kings because he had two horns, which are the ten-horned beast and the false prophet. The second beast in Revelation 13:11 and the fourth beast in Daniel 7:7–8 are the same beast. In Daniel, the ten horns made the fourth beast, and the little horn came up among them. The ten horns made one beast, and the little horn made another beast. So the second beast in Revelation had two kings and the fourth beast in Daniel had two kings: the ten-horned beast and the little-horned beast. It is important to keep in mind that a beast is a king. The ten-horned beast and the little-horned beast had one mind, so they then became one. The ten-horned beast will give its power and strength unto the little-horned beast, the false prophet They will become one beast.

Now, returning to the Antichrist's war on the saints, Daniel 7:25 reads, "And he shall speak great words against the most High, and shall wear out the saints of the most High, and think to change times and laws: and they shall be given into his hand until a time and times and the dividing of time." To gain further insight into the first part of this verse, "And he shall speak great words against the most High," we will turn to Isaiah 37:23; Daniel 8:24–25, 11:28, 11:30–31, and 11:36; and Revelation 13:5–6.

Isaiah 37:23 reads, "Whom hast thou reproached and blasphemed; and against whom hast thou exalted thy voice, and lifted up thine eyes on high? even against the Holy One of Israel." This passage shows that the Antichrist, the false prophet, will lift himself up against the Holy One, Jesus Christ.

Next, Daniel 8:24 reads, "And his power shall be mighty, but not by his own power: and he shall destroy wonderfully, and shall prosper, and practice, and shall destroy the mighty and the holy people." This means that the Antichrist's power will be mighty, but not by just his own power. His power will come from the power of the ten horns, the ten kings. He will come against the saints, which means he will come against God, the most High. Then verse 25 reads, "And through his policy also he shall cause craft to prosper in his hand; and he shall magnify himself in his heart, and by peace shall destroy many: he shall also stand up against the Prince of princes; but he shall be broken without hand." The passage, "he shall stand up against the prince of princes;" means the Antichrist will stand up against Jesus Christ.

Next, let's read from Daniel 11. Daniel 11:28 reads, "Then shall he return into his land with great riches; and his heart shall be against the holy covenant; and he shall do exploits, and return to his own land." This shows that the Antichrist will be against the holy covenant. That means he will be against Jesus Christ and against the saints. Next, Daniel 11:30 reads, "For the ships of Chittim shall come against him: therefore he shall be grieved, and return, and have indignation against the holy covenant: so shall he do; he shall even return, and have intelligence with them that forsake the holy covenant." The Antichrist will be against the Lord and the Lord's people. The false prophet will have intelligence with them that forsake the holy covenant. Intelligence means the ability to learn or understand. He will come against the saints.

Then Daniel 11:31 reads, "And arms shall stand on his part, and they shall pollute the sanctuary of strength, and shall take away the daily sacrifice, and they shall place the abomination that maketh desolate." This means armies will stand on the Antichrist's part, and they will pollute the church in Jerusalem. They will take away the daily sacrifice and kill and imprison the saints. The Antichrist will come against the holy covenant. He will kill the two witnesses and set up the abomination that maketh desolate. He will set up an image and want all people, languages, and nations to worship that image. You see, the daily sacrifice referenced Daniel 11:31 refers to the sacrifice of the saints of God, not animal sacrifices. In the new covenant of the New Testament, the saints are the daily sacrifice. So by taking away the sacrificed, the Antichrist will come against the holy covenant and against God and God's people.

Next let's read Daniel 11:36. It says, "And the king shall do according to his will; and he shall exalt himself, and magnify himself above every god, and shall speak marvelous things against the God of gods, and shall prosper till the indignation be accomplished: for that that is determined shall be done." The Antichrist shall speak marvelous things against God.

Now we turn to Revelation 13:5, which reads, "And there was given unto him a mouth speaking great things and blasphemies; and power was given unto him to continue forty and two months." As I have mentioned previously, the third beast had four heads, and one of his heads was wounded unto death. His deadly wound was healed, and after that he continued forty and two months. The false prophet was among the four heads of the third beast. The false prophet plucked up the other three heads of the beasts that were with him. He also had the ten horns with him. Therefore he made the second beast in the book of Revelation and the fourth beast in the book of Daniel.

Then Revelation 13:6 reads, "And he opened his mouth in blasphemy against God, to blaspheme has name, and his tabernacle, and them that dwell in heaven."

Next, let's return to Daniel 7:25, where it says, "wear out the saints of the most High," This means the Antichrist will be killing and imprisoning the saints of the most High. We find further clarification regarding this in Revelation 17:6 and 18:24. Revelation 17:6 reads, "And I saw the woman drunken with the blood of the saints, and with the blood of the martyrs of Jesus: and when I saw her, I wondered with great admiration." The woman stands for the church, the Roman Catholic Church and all the other false churches, the Vatican, the pope, and the false prophet. The woman—the church and the Antichrist—will kill the saints.

Next we read Revelation 18:24: "And in her was fund the blood of prophets, and of saints, and of all that were slain upon the earth." This passage illustrates that the church will shed the blood of the saints until she is drunk with it, drunk with the blood of the martyrs of Jesus. The Roman Catholic Church appears to be righteous, but they are unrighteous.

Going back once more to Daniel 7:25, we can further interpret the phrase "think to change times and laws:" with information from Daniel 2:21. It reads, "And he changeth the times and the seasons; he removeth kings, and setteth up kings; he giveth wisdom unto the wise, and knowledge to them that know understanding:". Praise the Lord. The Antichrist will think to change the times and laws because the ten kings will receive their power one hour with the beast. He will give the ten kings power to rule the world.

Let's now look at where Daniel 7:25 says, "they shall be given into his hand" Going to Revelation 13:7, we can see where the power is given to the third beast in this verse. It reads, "And it was given unto him to make war with the saints, and to overcome them: and power was given him over all kindreds, and tongues, and nations." This passage shows that the power will be given unto the third beast's hand to make war with the saints.

Now look at the last portion of Daniel 7:25: "until a time and times and the dividing of time." A "time" is the equivalent of one year, and "times" is the equivalent of two. The "dividing of time" is the equivalent of half a year, or six months. Those amounts of time combined equal three and a half years. That is how long the Antichrist will take control over Jerusalem.

Additional references to a three-and-a-half-year reign are mentioned in both the book of Daniel and Revelation. Daniel 12:7 reads, "And I heard the man clothed in linen, which was upon the waters of the river, when he held up his right hand and his left hand unto heaven, and sware by him that liveth for ever that it shall be for a time, times, and an half; and when he shall have accomplished to scatter the power of the holy people, all these things shall be finished." Notice the reference to three and a half years, and that's when the Antichrist will set up the image. The people in Judea will have to flee into the mountains. That's when the Lord will scatter the power of the holy people, in the last three and a half years when the Antichrist will set up his image and it will make the abomination that maketh desolate.

Now Revelation 12:14 reads, "And to the woman were given two wings of a great eagle, that she might fly into the wilderness, into her place, where she is nourished for a time, and times, and half a time, from the face of the serpent." The woman was given two wings of a great eagle. That means that the Lord will carry his people and bear them on the eagle's wings into the wilderness where she is nourished for three and a half years from the face of the serpent. This is when the great tribulation will start, and that's when the "devil is come down unto you, having great wrath, because he knoweth that he hath but a short time." (Rev. 12:12). The devil will get into the man of sin, the false prophet. He will have great anger against the saints. He will kill the two witnesses and set up an image and that will make the abomination that maketh desolate.

The great tribulation will then start, and the saints will have to flee into the wilderness. Those that are in Judea will have to flee into the mountains. It will be a terrible time. Never again will there be a time like that. It will be severe persecution for the saints. A false prophet from South Carolina says that the great tribulation will last forty-five days, but that is not true. The great tribulation will last for three and a half years.

Now, returning to the book of Daniel, Daniel 7:26 reads, "But the judgment shall sit, and they shall take away his dominion to consume and to destroy it unto the end." This means that the saints shall take the kingdom away from the Antichrist. Then Daniel 7:27 reads, "And the kingdom and dominion, and the greatness of the kingdom under the whole heaven, shall be given to the people of the saints of the most High, whose kingdom is an everlasting kingdom, and all dominions shall serve and obey him."

Finally, Daniel 7:28 reads, "Hitherto is the end of the matter. As for me Daniel, my cogitations much troubled me, and my countenance changed in me: but I kept the matter in my heart."

DANIEL 8

Now we will focus our attention on the next chapter of the book of Daniel. Daniel 8:1 reads, "In the third year of the reign of king Belshazzar a vision appeared unto me, even unto me Daniel, after that which appeared unto me at the first." Daniel had a vision appear to him like the vision in Daniel 7. Remember, Daniel 7:1 said, "In the first year of Belshazzar king of Babylon, Daniel had a dream and visions of his head, upon his bed: then he wrote the dream, and told the sum of the matters." Daniel 7 told about the first through the fourth beasts.

Daniel 8:2 goes on to tell about Daniel's second dream. It reads, "And I saw in a vision; and it came to pass, when I saw, that I was at Shushan in the palace, which is in the province of Elam; and I saw in a vision, and I was by the river of Ulai." I have heard people say that the river of Ulai runs through what is present-day Iraq. Where the verse says, "Shushan in the palace, which is in the province of Elam;" it simply means that Daniel was in Shushan when he saw the vision.

Daniel 8:3 reads, "Then I lifted up mine eyes, and saw, and behold, there stood before the river a ram which had two horns: and the two horns were high; but one was higher than the other, and the higher came up last." The two horns of the ram are symbols for the kings of Media and Persia, which are present-day Iraq and Iran. Iraq's horn has now been broken by the United States, the he goat. The higher horn came up last, and it stands for Iran. Iran is stronger than Iraq. So from this passage, we can interpret that Iran is next to be broken by the United States. Then, after breaking Iran's horn, the United States (the he-goat) his horn will be broken.

Now, moving on to Daniel 8:4, it reads, "I saw the ram pushing westward, and northward, and southward; so that no beasts might stand before him, neither was there any that could deliver out of his hand; but he did according to his will, and became great." The ram stands for the Arab people, who are making terrorism all over the world. They push westward and northward and southward so that no beast stands before him.

Next, Daniel 8:5 reads, "And as I was considering, behold, a he-goat came from the west on the face of the whole earth, and touched not the ground: and the goat had a notable horn between his eyes." The he-goat came from the west on the face of the whole earth and did not touch the ground. The he-goat is the United States, which is also known as the West, and when the United States forces went to Iraq, they did not touch the ground. They went on airplanes and by ship. The United States also has a notable horn between its eyes because it is known as a "super power." It is known for its military might, and everybody can see its notable horn.

Further clarification of Daniel 8:5 where it says, "a notable horn between his eyes." can be found in Daniel 8:21. It reads, "And the rough goat is the king of Grecia: and the great horn that is between his eyes is the first king." This is George Bush. Bush is the first king in that kingdom.

Continuing with Daniel's dream, Daniel 8:6 reads, "And he came to the ram that had two horns, which I had seen standing before the river, and ran unto him in the fury of his power." The United States ran to Iraq in the fury of his power. The he-goat will do the same thing to Iran. He will run into him in the fury of his power. He ran into him in anger. The he-goat has anger against Iraq and Iran.

Then Daniel 8:7 says, "And I saw him come close unto the ram, and he was moved with choler against him, and smote the ram, and brake his two horns: and there was no power in the ram to stand before him, but he cast him down to the ground, and stamped upon him: and there was none that could deliver the ram out of his hand." The ram is Iraq and Iran. The he-goat is angry with Iraq and Iran. So the he-goat will break the two horns: Iran and Iraq. They will have no power to stand before the United States. The he-goat will cast them down to the ground. Iran is next to be broken. Nobody will help Iran because nobody can deliver Iraq or Iran out of the he-goat's hand.

Daniel 8:8 then reads, "Therefore, the he-goat waxed very great: and when he was strong, the great horn was broken; and for it, came up four notable ones toward the four winds of heaven." For further clarification of the phrase, "four notable ones toward the four winds of heaven." we turn to Daniel 7:6, Daniel 11:4, and Daniel 8:22.

Daniel 7:6 reads, "After this, I beheld, and lo, another, like a leopard, which had upon the back of it four wings of a fowl: the beast had also four heads; and dominion was given to it." As we covered earlier, the third beast (the leopard), had four heads. The Antichrist, also known as the false prophet, came out from one of the four heads. But before the Antichrist shows up, the second beast will come. The second beast is Russia. After the second beast, then come the third beast. After the Antichrist comes out from one of the four heads of the third beast, he will get with the ten horns and make the fourth beast in Daniel and the second beast in Revelation 13:11.

Now Daniel 11:4 reads, "And when he shall stand up, his kingdom shall be broken, and shall be divided toward the four winds of heaven; and not to his posterity, nor according to his dominion which he ruled: for his kingdom shall be plucked up, even for others beside those." This means the United States' horn will be broken and divided. The four kings of the third beast will stand up for its four kingdoms. The kingdom of the United States will be plucked up even for others besides those. It means others besides the four kingdoms.

Finally, Daniel 8:22 reads, "Now that being broken, whereas four stood up for it, four kingdoms shall stand up out of the nation, but not in is power." So this means, after the United States' horn is broken, four kings will stand up out of the United Nation, but not in the power of the he goat, the United States.

Returning to Daniel's second dream, Daniel 8:9 reads, "And out of one of them came forth a little horn, which waxed exceeding great, toward the south, and toward the east, and toward the pleasant land." This means that out of one of the four notable ones came forth a little horn. The little horn stands for the false prophet, which is also the pope, who will come in at the end time and cause the two witnesses to be killed. After they are killed, he will set up the abomination that maketh desolate. He will set up an image, an image of the first beast—the beast that was wounded by a sword but lived (Rev. 13). The false prophet will make an image of the head that was wounded. He will want all people, tongues, and nations to worship the image or they should be killed. That little horn will wax exceeding great, even to the host of heaven.

We can find further evidence that the little horn refers to the Antichrist in Daniel 7:8 and Daniel 11:21. Daniel 7:8 reads, "I considered the horns, and behold there came up among them another little horn, before whom here were three of the first horns plucked up by the roots: and behold, in this horn were eyes like the eyes of man, and a mouth speaking great things." Daniel 11:21 reads, "And in his estate shall stand up a vile person, to whom they shall not give the honor of the kingdom: but he shall come in peaceably, and obtain the kingdom by flatteries." These passages speak of the Antichrist, the false prophet, the man of sin.

Next, Daniel 8:10 reads, "And it waxed great, even to the host of heaven; and it cast down some of the host and of the stars to the ground, and stamped upon them." The phrase, "And it waxed great," means to increase in riches. Additional details regarding this phrase can be found in Daniel 11:28: "Then shall he return into his land with great riches; and his heart shall be against the holy covenant; and he shall do exploits, and return to his own land." This passage also shows that horn will come against the holy covenant. He will come against Jesus Christ and the saints.

Now let's look more closely at the portion of Daniel 8:10 where it says, "the host of heaven." For more information, we turn to Isaiah 14:13. It reads, "For thou hast said in thine heart, I will ascend into heaven, I will exalt my throne above the stars of God: I will sit also upon the mount of the congregation, in the sides of the north:". This passage shows that Satan is the person doing all the talking. He wants to exalt his throne above the stars of God and sit upon the mount of the congregation. Today, Satan has taken over most of people's lives. They are trapped and snared by Satan and his demons, the fallen angels.

Now, returning to the next portion of Daniel 8:10, let's focus on the phrase, "it cast down some of the host and of the stars to the ground, and stamped upon them." Further clarification on this phrase can be found in Revelation 12:4. It reads, "And his tail drew the third part of the stars of heaven, and did cast them to the earth: and the dragon stood before the woman which was ready to be delivered, for to devour her child as soon as it was born." The stars represent the angels and the tail stands for the false prophet—the Antichrist, the man of sin—who will cause the people to be killed. His tail drew the third part of the stars of heaven. If you believe in false teachings, fallen angels (demons) will come down and get inside you, which will destroy you.

The Bible says, "for the devil is come down unto you, having great wrath, because he knoweth that he hath but a short time" (Rev. 12:12). This is the start of the great tribulation, which will last three and a half years before Jesus Christ returns.

Now, moving on to Daniel 8:11, the passage reads, "Yea, he magnified himself even to the prince of the host, and by him the daily sacrifice was taken away, and the place of his sanctuary was cast down." More information on the phrase, "he magnified himself"can be found in Jeremiah 48:26 and 48:42 and Daniel 11:36 and 8:25. For all the verses not listed below, you can read on your own. Daniel 8:25 reads, "And through his policy also he shall cause craft to prosper in his hand; and he shall magnify himself in his heart, and by peace shall destroy many: he shall also stand up against the Prince of princes; but he shall be broken without hand." This passage shows that the Antichrist magnified himself and stood up against the prince, Jesus Christ. The Antichrist will stand up against Jesus Christ, and though he will say there is peace, he will destroy many. People will hope for peace, but will be none.

Next let's look at the phrase in Daniel 8:11 that reads, "the prince of the host." The prince of the host is Jesus Christ. We can find more regarding this in Joshua 5:14. It reads, "And he said, Nay; but as captain of the host of the LORD am I now come. And Joshua fell on his face to the earth, and did worship, and said unto him, What saith my lord unto his servant?" In this passage, the captain of the host is Jesus Christ. Jesus Christ came as a man to Joshua and Abraham in the Old Testament.

In Genesis 18:2, Jesus Christ is God manifest in the flesh because angels look like man. In Genesis 1:26-27, "And God said, Let us make man in our image, after our likeness:" So this means that man looks like God and the angels. So when Jesus Christ came, he looked like a man and was God manifest in the flesh. Jesus Christ came to talk to Abraham in Genesis 18:2. There were three men, and they were angels. One of them was God, Jesus Christ. Genesis 18:22 confirms it was Jesus Christ. It reads, "And the men turned their faces from thence, and went toward Sodom: but Abraham stood yet before the LORD." The two men who turned their faces away were two angels who went toward Sodom. Abraham stood before Jesus Christ.

Now, returning to Daniel 8:11 where it says, "and by him the daily sacrifice was taken away, and the place of his sanctuary was cast down." let's divide the word of truth. It means by him, the Antichrist, the daily sacrifice shall be taken away. Further clarification on this phrase can be found in Daniel 11:31 and 12:11. For the verses not listed below, you can read on your own. Daniel 11:31 reads, "And arms shall stand on his part, and they shall pollute the sanctuary of strength, and shall take away the daily sacrifice, and they shall place the abomination that maketh desolate." This means he will kill and imprison the saints. As I previously mentioned, some prophets, preachers, and teachers believed that the daily sacrifice is animal sacrifices, but that is not true. The daily sacrifice is the saints of God in the New Testament, the new covenant. Romans 12:1 says, "I BESEECH you therefore, brethren, by the mercies of God, that ye present your bodies a living sacrifice, holy, acceptable unto God, which is your reasonable service." You see, In the New Testament, we present our bodies as a living sacrifice acceptable unto God. Daniel's prophecy was for the future, for the end of time. In the New Testament, the daily sacrifice is the saints of God. This is why the Antichrist will make war with the saints.

If Daniel's prophecy had been for the Old Testament, the sacrifice would have been animal sacrifices. We can turn to Exodus 29:38; Numbers 28:3; and Ezekiel 46:13 for additional evidence. These verses pertain to animal sacrifice. Exodus 29:38 reads, "Now this is that which thou shalt offer upon the altar; two lambs of the first year day by day continually." This verse shows the animal sacrifice of the Old Testament. They had to offer sacrifice up to the Lord continually, day by day, in the Old Testament. In the New Testament, the saints are the daily sacrifice.

Now we turn to Numbers 28:3: "And thou shalt say unto them, This is the offering made by fire which ye shall offer unto the LORD; two lambs of the first year without spot day by day, for a continual burnt offering." They had to offer one lamb in the morning and one in the evening. This was the daily sacrifice in the Old Testament under the first covenant, but Daniel's prophecy was for the end time and we are now under the new covenant or the New Testament. Under the new covenant, the saints of God are the daily sacrifice. You can read Ezekiel 46:13 on your own for additional proof.

Let us return once again to Daniel's second dream. Daniel 8:12 reads, "And a host was given him against the daily sacrifice by reason of transgression, and it cast down the truth to the ground; and it practiced, and prospered." This means an army was given to the Antichrist against the daily sacrifice, against the saints.

Now, focusing on the phrase, "a host was given him against the daily sacrifice by reason of transgression," we can further interpret it with Daniel 11:31. It reads, "And arms shall stand on his part, and they shall pollute the sanctuary of strength, and shall take away the daily sacrifice, and they shall place the abomination that maketh desolate." This talks about when they will take away the daily sacrifice and kill the two witnesses and make war with the saints. They will place the abomination that maketh desolate, which means the Antichrist, the false prophet, will set up an image of the beast and want all the people, nations, and tongues to worship it. That is when the great tribulation will start.

Now let's look more closely at where Daniel 8:12 says, "the truth to the ground." We turn to Psalm 119:43 and 119:142 and Isaiah 59:14 for more information. Psalms 119:43 reads, "And take not the word of truth utterly out of my mouth; for I have hoped in thy judgments." The Antichrist will cast down the truth. He will make war with the saints and not the animals because the saints will have the truth and animals do not. Animal sacrifices were done away with when Christ died on the cross for our sins.

Psalms 119:142 reads, "Thy righteousness is an everlasting righteousness, and thy law is the truth." The Antichrist will cast down the truth, and he will try to take away God's law. He will cast down the truth. We can see this happening today. The law of God is being taken away from the people. The people don't know the law of God anymore. The pastors are not telling and explaining the law of God to the people. The Antichrist will think to change times and laws, and it is happening now. Laws such as women's rights, homosexual rights, children's rights, and on and on are being changed. You can no longer talk about Jesus in public places.

Finally, Isaiah 59:14 reads, "And judgment is turned away backward, and justice standeth afar off: for truth is fallen in the street, and equity cannot enter." We can see evidence of this in the world today. We don't have justice in the land anymore. For example, when a woman commits the same crime as a man, he will receive a longer jail sentence. He will get twenty or thirty years, and she might get two years or probation. There is no more justice. The power of the men has diminished. A man is supposed to be the head, but now women are ruling over him. The truth has fallen into the street. The justice system no longer stands for the truth. And it will get worse. The Antichrist will come and try to cast down the truth and all of God's laws.

Now Daniel 8:13 reads, "Then I heard one saint speaking, and another saint said unto that certain saint which spake, How long shall be the vision concerning the daily sacrifice, and the transgression of desolation, to give both the sanctuary and the host to be trodden under foot?" This passage shows that the churches' lights are going out. They are starting to be trodden underfoot.

Now divide the verse where it says, "one saint speaking, and another saint said unto that certain saint which spake,". That certain saint is Jesus Christ. We can see further proof of this in Daniel 4:13 and 12:6 and 1 Peter 1:12.

Daniel 4:13 reads, "I saw in the visions of my head upon my bed, and behold, a watcher and an holy one came down from heaven." I believe the holy one is Jesus Christ. Then Daniel 12:6 reads, "And one said to the man clothed in linen, which was upon the waters of the river, How long shall it be to the end of these wonders?" The one clothed in linen is Jesus Christ. Next, 1 Peter 1:12 says, "Unto whom it was revealed, that not unto themselves, but unto us they did minister the things which are now reported unto you by them that have preached the gospel unto you, with the Holy Ghost sent down from heaven; which things the angels desire to look into." This means that the angels desire to look into when the Holy Ghost came down, the apostle went and preached the gospel into all nations.

Now, moving on to Daniel 8:14, it reads, "And he said unto me, Unto two thousand and three hundred days: then shall the sanctuary be cleansed." Two thousand and three hundred days is about six years. The Antichrist will come into power before he sets up the abomination that maketh desolate. He comes in Daniel 11:21. If you read through the book of Daniel, you will see he made war with the king of the south. In Daniel 11:31, he took away the daily sacrifice. He will kill the two witnesses, make war with the saints, and then he will set up the abomination that maketh desolate. After these events, Jerusalem will then go into captivity for three and a half years. During that time, Jerusalem shall be trodden down by the gentiles.

Next, Daniel 8:15 reads, "And it came to pass, when I, even I Daniel, had seen the vision, and sought for the meaning, then behold, there stood before me as the appearance of a man." The meaning of the phrase, "sought for the meaning" can be interpreted by Daniel 12:8 and 1 Peter 1:10–11. Daniel 12:8 reads, "And I heard, but I understood not: then said I, O my Lord, what shall be the end of these things?" This verse shows that Daniel heard, but he didn't understand.

Then 1 Peter 1:10 reads, "Of which salvation the prophets have inquired and searched diligently, who prophesied of the grace that should come unto you:" The prophets inquired and searched diligently because they wanted to know when Jesus Christ would come. First

Peter 1:11 then reads, "Searching what, or what manner of time, the Spirit of Christ which was in them did signify, when it testified beforehand the sufferings of Christ, and the glory that should follow."

Now, returning to Daniel's dream, Daniel 8:16 reads, "And I heard a man's voice between the banks of Ulai, which called, and said, Gabriel, make this man to understand the vision." First, to clarify the identity of the man who speaks, let's back up to Daniel 8:15 once more where it says, "as the appearance of a man." The man is Jesus Christ. Ezekiel 1:26 reads, "And above the firmament that was over their heads was the likeness of a throne, as the appearance of a sapphire stone: and upon the likeness of the throne was the likeness as the appearance of a man above upon it." It was Jesus Christ upon the throne in heaven.

We can gain further insight into the phrase, "between the banks of Ulai" (Dan. 8:16), in Daniel 12:6–7. Daniel 12:6 reads, "And one said to the man clothed in linen, which was upon the waters of the river, How long shall it be to the end of these wonders?" The man clothed in linen is Jesus Christ. He told Gabriel to help make Daniel understand the vision (Ezek 1:26). Next, verse 7 reads, "And I heard the man clothed in linen, which was upon the waters of the river, when he held up his right hand and his left hand unto heaven, and sware by him that liveth for ever, that it shall be for a time, times, and an half; and when he shall have accomplished to scatter the power of the holy people, all these things shall be finished." In these two verses, Jesus was upon the waters of the river and the other two angels were on opposite banks of the river. One asked Jesus how long it will be before the end. He said it will be for a time, times, and a half, which is three and a half years. That is how long the Antichrist shall rule after he sets up the abomination that maketh desolate. The image is what will start the great tribulation and it will last for three and a half years.

Looking more closely at where Daniel 12:7 says, "And when he shall have accomplished to scatter the power of" we look to Luke 21:24 and Revelation 10:7 for further clarification. God will scatter the power of the holy people. He will use men to do it. He will allow the Antichrist to do it. However, it is actually God who will scatter the power of the holy people during the great tribulation.

Luke 21:24 reads, "And they shall fall by the edge of the sword, and shall be led away captive into all nations: and Jerusalem shall be trodden down of the Gentiles, until the times of the Gentiles be fulfilled." Some of the people in Jerusalem will be killed, and some will be scattered into all nations. The great tribulation will then start. Next, Revelation 10:7 reads, "But in the days of the voice of the seventh angel, when he shall begin to sound, the mystery of God should be finished, as he hath declared to his servants the prophets." I believe this verse talks about the great tribulation, and Jesus Christ will come back.

Now let's turn back where Daniel 8:16 says, "Gabriel, make this man to understand the vision." From here we turn to Daniel 9:21 and Luke 1:19 and 1:26. For the verses not listed below, you can read on your own. Daniel 9:21 reads, "Yea, while I was speaking in prayer, even the man Gabriel, whom I had seen in the vision at the beginning, being caused to fly swiftly, touched me about the time of the evening oblation." This confirms that the Lord wanted Gabriel to make Daniel understand the vision of the end time.

Moving forward with Daniel's dream, Daniel 8:17 reads, "So he came near where I stood: and when he came, I was afraid, and fell upon my face: but he said unto me, Understand, O son of man: for at the time of the end shall be the vision." The angel, Gabriel, tried to make Daniel understand that the vision of the time of the end. Now let's focus on the phrase "fell upon my face." Corresponding passages occur in the book of Ezekiel and Revelation.

Ezekiel 1:28 reads, "As the appearance of the bow that is in the cloud in the day of rain, so was the appearance of the brightness round about. This was the appearance of the likeness of the glory of the LORD. And when I saw it, I fell upon my face, and I heard a voice of one that spake." Revelation 1:17 reads, "And when I saw him, I fell at his feet as dead. And he laid his right hand upon me, saying unto me, Fear not; I am the first and the last:". These passages show that the saints of God always fall upon their faces instead of their backs. They do not fall backward like Judas, the chief priests, and the Pharisees. Daniel also fell upon his face.

Now Daniel 8:18 reads, "Now as he was speaking with me, I was in a deep sleep on my face toward the ground: but he touched me, and set me upright." Let's look more closely at the meaning of the phrase, "Now as he was speaking with me, I was in a deep sleep on my face toward the ground:". For this we turn to Daniel 10:9–10 and Luke 9:32. For the verses not listed below, you can read on your own.

Daniel 10:9 reads, "Yet heard I the voice of his words: and when I heard the voice of his words, then was I in a deep sleep on my face, and my face toward the ground." This shows that Daniel was in a deep sleep when the angel told him about the end time. Then Daniel 10:10 reads, "And behold, an hand touched me, which set me upon my knees and upon the palms of my hands."

Now let's look at the part of Daniel 8:18 that says, "but he touched me, and set me upright." Further clarification for this phrase can be found in the book of Ezekiel. Ezekiel 2:2 reads, "And the spirit entered into me when he spake unto me, and set me upon my feet, that I heard him that spake unto me." So after Daniel slept, he stood upon his feet.

Moving on, Daniel 8:19 reads, "And he said, Behold, I will make thee know what shall be in the last end of the indignation: for at the time appointed the end shall be." In this verse, the angel is telling Daniel about the end time. Further information on the phrase, "for at the time appointed end shall be." can be found in Daniel 9:27, 11:27, 11:35, 11:36, and 12:7, as well as Habakkuk 2:3.

I will explain Daniel 9:27 and invite you to read the rest of the verses on your own. Daniel 9:27 reads, "And he shall confirm the covenant with many for one week: and in the midst of the week he shall cause the sacrifice and the oblation to cease, and for the overspreading of abominations, he shall make it desolate, even until the consummation, and that determined shall be poured upon the desolate." In this verse, the Bible is talking about the last seven years, the end time. Where it says, "And he shall confirm the covenant with many for one week:" the "he" is Jesus Christ. Jesus will confirm the covenant with many for one week.

The Lord will give power unto his two witnesses. The saints, the elect, will know that God is with the two witnesses. That is when the Lord will confirm the covenant with many for one week. Like it says in Daniel 12, many shall be made white, and in the midst of the week he shall cause the sacrifice and the oblation to cease. That's when the two witnesses shall be killed and the daily sacrifice taken away. When they kill the witnesses, they will make war with the saints. The second beast, the false prophet, in Revelation will kill the two witnesses, and the Antichrist will last for three and a half years.

Moving on to Daniel 8:20, it reads, "The ram which thou sawest having two horns are the kings of Media and Persia." The ram is Media and Persia, which is the same as Iraq and Iran. In present-day, Iraq has already been destroyed and Iran is next. The image of the ram also occurs in Daniel 8:3, which reads, "Then I lifted up mine eyes, and saw, and behold, there stood before the river a ram which had two horns: and the two horns were high; but one was higher than the other, and the higher came up last." The reference to the higher horn is Iran. The United States, the he-goat from the west, broke Iraq's horn first and will break Iran's horn next.

Next, Daniel 8:21 reads, "And the rough goat is the king of Grecia: and the great horn that is between his eyes is the first king." The rough goat is the global opposition against terrorism. That's where the word goat came from. The United States is fighting war against terrorism around the world. At the end time, the king of Grecia is the he-goat. He is the first of the seven kings that will rule the beast government at the end time.

Further clarification on the first portion of 8:21, "And the rough goat is the king of Grecia:" can be found in Daniel 8:5. It reads, "And as I was considering, behold, a he-goat came from the west on the face of the whole earth, and touched not the ground: and the goat had a notable horn between his eyes." The he-goat came from the west, which is a symbol for the United States. The United States went over to Iraq the army by airplane and boat and therefore did not touch the ground. That was the first trumpet (hail, fire mingle with blood).

If we continue forward, Daniel 8:22 reads, "Now that being broken, whereas four stood up for it, four kingdoms shall stand up out of the nation, but not in his power." This means that after the United States' horn is broken, four kingdoms out of the United Nations will stand up for it. The Antichrist will come from one of the four. Some of the false prophets, teachers, and preachers of today believe that the antichrist was President Bush of the United States. However, that is not true because the United States' horn will be plucked up. Four shall stand up out of the nation. This refers to the United Nations, but they will not stand up in the he-goat's power because his horn is broken.

Then Daniel 8:23 reads, "And in the latter time of their kingdom, when the transgressors are come to the full, a king of fierce countenance, and understanding dark sentences, shall stand up." The third beast with four heads will stay in power for a while, probably eight to ten years or longer. Then the Antichrist will come out of one of the four and join the ten horns, which are also called the ten kings. This will make the fourth beast mentioned in Daniel and the second beast in Revelation. When the transgressors come to the full, the Antichrist will take over and pluck up the other three beasts. Then, as explained previously, he will kill the two witnesses and set up the abomination that maketh desolate. Jerusalem will then go into captivity for three and a half years.

Next, Daniel 8:24 reads, "And his power shall be mighty, but not by his own power: and he shall destroy wonderfully, and shall prosper, and practise, and shall destroy the mighty and the holy people." The passage "And his power shall be mighty, but not by his own power:" means the Antichrist will have power from the ten horns, the ten kings. As I mentioned earlier, false prophets, teachers, and preachers in modern times think the little horn is the he-goat, the United States, but that is not true. The little horn is the false prophet.

Now let's take a closer look at the phrase "but not by his own power:". Further clarification can be found in the book of Revelation. Revelation 17:13 reads, "These have one mind, and shall give their power and strength unto the beast." These ten kings shall give their power to the false prophet. This is the equivalent of the Roman Catholic Church and the other false churches teaching false doctrine. People are following doctrine of men and cannot see the truth because they are blind. God is sending them a strong delusion. They believe a lie because they do not love the truth.

Offering even further evidence, Revelation 17:17 reads, "For God hath put in their hearts to fulfill his will, and to agree, and give their kingdom unto the beast, until the words of God shall be fulfilled." The ten kings will destroy the whore churches. That what you will read about in Revelation 18:8. Today, the churches are polluted. The false prophet is the head of these churches, and they are everywhere. People have to come out of them. Organized religions are doctrine of men. The false prophet shall destroy wonderfully, and by peace he shall destroy many. He will say the destruction and death are the people's doing. He will say he wants peace, like what is going on in Iraq now. It was suppose to be an act of peace and democracy, but the people are being killed. They will say they want peace, but there is none.

Now, returning to Daniel 8:24, to find more information about where it says, "and shall prosper, and practise," we turn to Daniel 8:12 and 11:36. Daniel 8:12 reads, "And a host was given him against the daily sacrifice by reason of transgression, and it cast down the truth to the ground; and it practised, and prospered." This passage says the Antichrist prospered.

The next focusing on where it says, "and shall destroy the mighty and the holy people" (Da. 8:24), we turn to Daniel 8:10 and 7:25. Daniel 8:10 reads, "And it waxed great, even to the host of heaven; and it cast down some of the host and of the stars to the ground, and stamped upon them." The passage shows that the Antichrist waxed great, even to the host of heaven. The host of heaven means the angels. the host of heaven The Antichrist will destroy the mighty and the holy people—the saints. Then, Daniel 7:25 reads, "And he shall speak great words against the most High, and shall wear out the saints of the most High, and think to change times and laws: and they shall be given into his hand until a time and times and the dividing of time." And this passage, "And shall wear out the saints of the most High," means the Antichrist will kill the saints of the most High.

Moving on, Daniel 8:25 reads, "And through his policy also he shall cause craft to prosper in his hand; and he shall magnify himself in his heart, and by peace shall destroy many: he shall also stand up against the Prince of princes; but he shall be broken without hand." To gain further insight into where it says, "through his policy also he shall cause craft to prosper in his hand;" we turn to Daniel chapter 11:21 and 11:23–24.

Daniel 11:21 reads, "And in his estate shall stand up a vile person, to whom they shall not give the honor of the kingdom: but he shall come in peaceably, and obtain the kingdom by flatteries." This means he will come in peaceably, talking peace as if he were kind. He will flatter the people, but he is a vile person, a wicked and evil man. It is much like when a boy meets a girl. He will talk nice and peaceful like he is a nice boy, but underneath he is a wicked person. She will find out later that he is not as nice. The Antichrist will come in peaceably, but by peace he shall destroy many. He will say he wants peace in the region, but all the while, he will be killing people, much like what is happening in the world today

Daniel 11:23–24 offers additional clarification. Daniel 11:23 reads, "And after the league made with him he shall work deceitfully: for he shall come up, and shall become strong with a small people." You see, after the ten kings give the Antichrist their power, he will work deceitfully and destroy many by peace. Next, Daniel 11:24 reads, "He shall enter peaceably even upon the fattest places of the province; and he shall do that which his fathers have not done, nor his fathers' fathers; he shall scatter among them the prey, and spoil, and riches: yea, and he shall forecast his devices against the strong holds, even for a time." This means he will take an abundance of things by attack, and he shall prosper. Remember, beasts will attack you at night. That is why warring nations always attach other nations at night. Then the Antichrist will stand up against the prince of princes; which is Jesus Christ.

Daniel 8:26 then reads, "And the vision of the evening and the morning which was told is true: wherefore shut thou up the vision; for it shall be for many days." Focusing on the first part of this verse, "And the vision of the evening and the morning which was told is true:" let's turn to Daniel 10:1. It reads, "In the third year of Cyrus king of Persia a thing was revealed unto Daniel, whose name was called Belteshazzar; and the thing was true, but the time appointed was long: and he understood the thing, and had understanding of the vision." This passage shows that the time between the dream and when it would come to pass was long and confirms that the vision was of the end time. The vision is true, and we are now at the end time.

Finally, Daniel 8:27 reads, "And I Daniel fainted, and was sick certain days; afterward I rose up, and did the king's business; and I was astonished at the vision, but none understood it."

DANIEL 12

Daniel 12:1 reads, "And at that time shall Michael stand up, the great prince which standeth for the children of thy people: and there shall be a time of trouble, such as never was since there was a nation even to that same time: and at that time thy people shall be delivered, every one that shall be found written in the book." This passage shows when the great tribulation will start. It will be a time of trouble such that has not been known since there was a nation.

We can find further clarification for the first part of the verse that reads, "Michael stand up, the great prince which standeth for the children of thy people:" in Daniel 10. Daniel 10:13 reads, "But the prince of the kingdom of Persia withstood me one and twenty days: but lo, Michael, one of the chief princes, came to help me; and I remained there with the kings of Persia." One of the chief angels, Michael, came to help Daniel. Then, if we jump to Daniel 10:21, it reads, "But I will show thee that which is noted in the scripture of truth: and there is none that holdeth with me in these things, but Michael your prince." Michael is the great prince "which standeth for the children of thy people:" (Dan. 12:1).

Additional information on the second part of Daniel 12:1, which says "and there shall be a time of trouble, such as never was since there was a nation even to that same time:" can be found in the books of Isaiah, Jeremiah, Matthew, and Revelation.

Isaiah 26:20 reads, "Come, my people, enter thou into thy chambers, and shut thy doors about thee: hide thyself as it were for a little moment, until the indignation be overpast." This verse shows the start of the great tribulation. Isaiah 26:21 then reads, "For behold, the LORD cometh out of his place to punish the inhabitants of the earth for their iniquity: the earth also shall disclose her blood, and shall no more cover her slain." This means the Lord will slaughter many in great numbers because of the sin of the people. It is starting to happen right now. We are in the beginning of the sorrow during the great tribulation. The Lord will punish the inhabitants of the earth.

Next, Jeremiah 30:7 reads, "Alas! For that day is great, so that none is like it: it is even the time of Jacob's trouble, but he shall be saved out of it." The time of Jacob's trouble stands for the great tribulation. Then, Matthew 24:21 reads, "For then shall be great tribulation, such as was not since the beginning of the world to this time, no, nor ever shall be." The great tribulation will start when they set up the image and want everyone to worship it. During that time, no man will be able to buy or sell "save he that had the mark, or the name of the beast, or the number of his name" (Rev. 13:17). Finally, Revelation 16:18 reads, "And there were voices, and thunders, and lightnings; and there was a great earthquake, such as was not since men were upon the earth, so mighty an earthquake, and so great." This shows what will happen before Jesus Christ comes back.

The final portion of Daniel 12:1 reads, "shall be delivered, every onethat shall be found written in the book." Additional information on the meaning of this phrase can be found in the book of Romans. Romans 11:26 reads, "And so all Israel shall be saved: as it is written, There shall come out of Sion the Deliverer, and shall turn away ungodliness from Jacob:" In this passage, Israel stands for everyone found written in the book. Israel is the Jews and Gentiles, the saint elect, who are the ones that will be saved.

Let's focus in for a moment on the phrase, "written in the book" (Dan. 12:1). We will turn to Exodus 32:32; Psalm 56:8; Psalm 69:28; Ezekiel 13:9;

Luke 10:20; Philippians 4:3; Revelation 3:5 and 13:8. For all the verses not mentioned below, you can read on your own.

Exodus 32:32 reads, "Yet now, if thou wilt forgive their sin: and if not, blot me, I pray thee, out of thy book which thou hast written." In this passage, Moses wanted the Lord to forgive the people for their sins, but if God did not, Moses wanted Him to blot out his name out of the book the Lord had written. Ezekiel 13:9 reads, "And mine hand shall be upon the prophets that see vanity, and that divine lies: they shall not be in the assembly of my people, neither shall they be written in the writing of the house of Israel, neither shall they enter into the land of Israel; and ye shall know that I am the Lord GOD." Here the Lord says the prophets that see vanity and divine lies will not enter into the land of Israel, and they won't be written in the writing of the house of Israel. The prophets of today keep changing what they say because they see vanity and tell lies. Things do not happen the way they claim. This is why they are angry. They have seen vanity and divine lies.

Revelation 13:8 reads, "And all that dwell upon the earth shall worship him, whose names are not written in the book of life of the Lamb slain from the foundation of the world." This passage means the people whose names are not written in the book of life will worship the beast.

Now let's continue to the next verse in Daniel 12. Daniel 12:2 reads, "And many of them that sleep in the dust of the earth shall awake, some to everlasting life, and some to shame and everlasting contempt." This verse means the ones that are in Christ will rise when Christ comes back. However, the ones that are not in Christ will rise after the thousand years.

Let's take a closer look at the phrase "some to everlasting life." For this we will turn to the books of Matthew, John, and Acts. First, Matthew 25:46 reads, "And these shall go away into everlasting punishment: but the righteous into life eternal." This says that, though everybody wants to be saved, only a few will be. Next, John 5:28–29 says, "Marvel not at this: for the hour is coming, in the which all that are in the graves shall hear his voice, And shall come forth; they that have done good, unto the resurrection of life; and they that have done evil, unto the resurrection of damnation." These verses show that everyone will rise eventually, but the dead in Christ will rise first. And finally, Acts 24:15 reads, "And have hope toward God, which they themselves also allow, that there shall be a resurrection of the dead, both of the just and unjust." This says again that the just will rise first when Christ returns. Then, after a thousand years, the unjust will rise to be judged.

Now let's go to the next portion of Daniel 12:2 where it says, "and everlasting contempt." For further insight into this phrase, we will look to the books of Isaiah and Romans. Isaiah 66:24 reads, "And they shall go forth, and look upon the carcases of the men that have transgressed against me: for their worm shall not die, neither shall their fire be quenched; and they shall be an abhorring unto all flesh." This verse shows what will happen to us if we don't repent for our sins: we will burn forever. Next, Romans 9:21 reads, "Hath not the potter power over the clay, of the same lump to make one vessel unto honour, and another unto dishonour?" This means God made some people unto honor and some unto dishonor, some people for his elect and some for destruction.

Moving forward with Daniel 12, verse 3 reads, "And they that be wise, shall shine as the brightness of the firmament; and they that turn many to righteousness, as the stars for ever and ever." Let's focus on the phrase "they that be wise, shall" for a moment. We will look to Daniel 11:33 and 11:35 for further explanation. Daniel 11:33 reads, "And they that understand among the people shall instruct many: yet they shall fall by the sword, and by flame, by captivity, and by spoil, many days." This passage says those who are wise will teach many, but some will be killed and some put in prison. Next, Daniel 11:35 reads, "And some of them of understanding shall fall. to try them, and to purge, and to make them white, even to the time of the end: because it is yet for a time appointed." This means some of the saints will die while trying to instruct many to make them white.

Let's focus on the next portion of Daniel 12:3, which reads, "shine as the brightness of the firmament." Here we will turn to the books of Proverbs and Matthew. Proverbs 4:18 reads, "But the path of the just is as the shining light, that shineth more and more unto the perfect day." It means the righteous shall shine as light. Matthew 13:43 reads, "Then shall the righteous shine forth as the sun in the kingdom of their Father. Who hath ears to hear, let him hear." This passage shows that the righteous will shine as the sun in the kingdom of God.

The next portion of Daniel 12:3 reads, "and they that turn many to righteousness." We will go to the book of James for further explanation. James 5:20 reads, "Let him know, that he which converteth the sinner from the error of his way shall save a soul from death, and shall hide a multitude of sins." This means if you convert a sinner from the error of his way you will save a soul from death.

Now let's return to Daniel 12:3 where the final portion says, "as the stars for ever and ever." The book of 1 Corinthians gives us further insight into this phrase. First Corinthians 15:41–42 reads, "There is one glory of the sun, and another glory of the moon, and another glory of the stars; for one star differeth from another star in glory. So also is the resurrection of the dead. It is sown in corruption, it is raised in incorruption:" This verse says the righteous will be as the stars forever and ever, and they will be remove and replace with: sun raised in incorruption. from the dead different from one another in glory.

Next, Daniel 12:4 reads, "But thou, O Daniel, shut up the words, and seal the book, even to the time of the end: many shall run to and fro, and knowledge shall be increased." This verse tells us that knowledge will be increased for the righteous, and the wicked will not retain any knowledge of God.

If we look further in depth at the phrase, "But thou, O Daniel," (Daniel 12:4), we turn to Daniel 8:26 and 12:9 for more clarification. Daniel 8:26 reads, "And the vision of the evening and the morning which was told is true: wherefore shut thou up the vision; for it shall be for many days." Daniel 12:9 reads, "And he said, Go thy way, Daniel: for the words are closed up and sealed till the time of the end." These verses reveal that the vision was shut up until the time of the end. But now that we are in the end time, the visions are being opened up once more to the righteous.

Now let's focus on the next portion of Daniel 12:4, which says, "shut up the words, and seal the book." Verses within the book of Revelation provide further insight. Revelation 10:4 reads, "And when the seven thunders had uttered their voices, I was about to write: and I heard a voice from heaven saying unto me, Seal up those things which the seven thunders uttered, and write them not." This is further evidence that Daniel's visions are sealed up until the time of the end. The seven thunders and uttered voices are the seven angels with seven trumpets. Then Revelation 22:10 reads, "And he saith unto me, Seal not the sayings of the prophecy of this book: for the time is at hand." This passage shows that the prophecy of the book is not sealed at the end time.

Now, we will return once again to Daniel 12:4. To learn more about the next portion of the verse, "the time of the end," we will read Daniel 10:1. It reads, "In the third year of Cyrus king of Persia a thing was revealed unto Daniel, whose name was called Belteshazzar; and the thing was true, but the time appointed was long: and he understood the thing, and had understanding of the vision." The phrase, "the time appointed was long" means his vision was of the end time.

Moving forward in the book of Daniel, Daniel 12:5 reads, "Then I Daniel looked, and behold, there stood other two, the one on this side of the bank of the river, and the other on that side of the bank of the river." Daniel saw two angels, each on opposite side of the banks of the river, and Jesus Christ was upon the waters of the river. The reference to the river in this verse also relates to Daniel 10:4, which reads, "And in the four and twentieth day of the first month, as I was by the side of the great river, which is Hiddekel." Jesus Christ was upon the great river, which is Hiddekel.

Next, Daniel 12:6 reads, "And one said to the other man clothed in linen, which was upon the waters of the river, How long shall it be to the end of these wonders?" Look closely at the words, "the man clothed in linen, which was upon the waters of the river." This passage relates to Daniel 10:5, which reads, "Then I lifted up mine eyes, and looked, and behold a certain man clothed in linen, whose loins were girded with fine gold of Uphaz:" In both instances, the man clothed in linen is Jesus Christ.

To gain further insight one of them ask Jesus how long would be to the end of the wonder.? we will turn back to Daniel 8:13, which mirrors this vision. It reads, "Then I heard one saint speaking, and another saint said unto that certain saint which spake, How long shall be the vision concerning the daily sacrifice, and the transgression of desolation, to give both the sanctuary and the host to be trodden under foot?" Keep in mind the angels are called saints, too, and the certain saint is Jesus.

Daniel 12:7 then reads, "And I heard the man clothed in linen, which was upon the waters of the river, when he held up his right hand and his left hand unto heaven, and sware by him that liveth for ever, that it shall be for a time, times, and an half; and when he shall have accomplished to scatter the power of the holy people, all these things shall be finished." As I said previously, the man clothed in linen is Jesus Christ.

We can find further insight into the phrase, "held up his right hand and his left hand unto heaven, and sware by him" in the book of Deuteronomy and Revelation. Deuteronomy 32:40 reads, "For I lift up my hand to heaven, and say, I live for ever." This shows there is only one Lord, one God. The Lord Jesus Christ and God are one in the same. Then, Revelation 10:5 reads, "And the angel which I saw stand upon the sea and upon the earth, lifted up his hand to heaven," The angel is Jesus Christ. And then Revelation 10:6 continues, "And sware by him that liveth for ever and ever, who created heaven, and the things that therein are, and the earth, and the things that therein are, and the sea, and the things which are therein, that there should be time no longer:" This verse is evidence that it all will be finished in the seventh trumpet.

Now let's look at the next part of Daniel 12:7 where it says, "that liveth for ever" Here we will turn to Daniel 4:34, which reads, "And at the end of the days I Nebuchadnezzar lifted up mine eyes unto heaven, and mine understanding returned unto me, and I blessed the most High, and I praised and honoured him that liveth for ever, whose dominion is an everlasting dominion, and his kingdom is from generation to generation:" This verse shows that the Lord Jesus Christ will live forever.

The next portion of Daniel 12:7, "that it shall be for a time, times and an half;" references the three-and-a-half-year period in which the Antichrist will make war with the saints. Additional insight into this portion of the verse can be found in Daniel 7 and 11.

Daniel 7:25 reads, "And he shall speak great words against the most High, and shall wear out the saints of the most High, and think to change times and laws: and they shall be given into his hand until a time and times and the dividing of time." This verse is talking about the Antichrist; he will do all of these things. He will speak great words against the most High for three and a half years. Then Daniel 11:13 reads, "For the king of the north shall return, and shall set forth a multitude greater than the former, and shall certainly come after certain years with a great army and with much riches." This verse says after a certain number of years, after a number of years, the king of the north will come with a great army.

Revelation 12:14 offers even more insight, still. It reads, "And to the woman were given two wings of a great eagle, that she might fly into the wilderness, into her place, where she is nourished for a time, and times, and half a time, from the face of the serpent." (the devil,) The church is the woman. She will have to flee into the wilderness from the serpent for three and a half years, and that will be the time of the great tribulation. The great tribulation begins in Revelation 12:12 where it says, "Wo to the inhabiters of the earth, and of the sea! for the devil is come down unto you, having great wrath, because he knoweth that he hath but a short time." This is when the Antichrist will make war with the saints. He will come against the holy covenant and God's people because God made a covenant with his people.

Let us turn to the next section of Daniel 12:7. For further clarification of the phrase, "and when he shall have accomplished to scatter the power of the holy people," we look to the books of Luke and Revelation. I will explain Luke 21:24 below and will let you read Revelation 10:7 on your own.

Luke 21:24 reads, "And they shall fall by the edge of the sword, and shall be led away captive into all nations: and Jerusalem shall be trodden down of the Gentiles, until the times of the Gentiles be fulfilled." This verse shows that some of the people in Jerusalem will fall by the edge of the sword, which means some will be killed by war, and some will be led away captive into all the nations and held for three and a half years. Then the Lord will go forth and fight against those nations, just as he fought the day of the battle when the nations came against Jerusalem. (Zechariah 14:3,16). This will be the battle of Armageddon. in the last days the Lord will scatter the power of the holy people for three and a half years, and the woman (the church) and the saints will flee into the wilderness from the serpent.

For next part of Daniel 12:7, "all these things shall be finished," we will refer to Daniel 8:24 for more information about the Antichrist "And his power shall be mighty, but not by his own power: and he shall destroy wonderfully, and shall prosper, and practise, and shall destroy the mighty and the holy people." His power will come from the ten horns, which are the ten kings. He will destroy the mighty and holy people. He will make war with the saints and kill and imprison them.

Next, Daniel 12:8 reads, "And I heard, but I understood not: then said I, O my Lord, what shall be the end of these things?" Daniel heard, but he did not understand because the Lord will only reveal the prophecy's meaning to his people at the end time. Only then will they understand.

Then Daniel 12:9 reads, "And he said, Go thy way, Daniel: for the words are closed up and sealed till the time of the end." If we look closely at where it says, "till the time of the end," we can turn back to Daniel 12:4 to help us interpret further meaning. It reads, "But thou, O Daniel, shut up the words, and seal the book, even to the time of the end: many shall run to and fro, and knowledge shall be increased." So, knowledge shall be increased for the righteous people but not for the wicked. The Bible says the following about the unrighteous: "Ever learning and never able to come to the knowledge of the truth" (2 Tim. 3:7).

Daniel 12:10 then reads, "Many shall be purified, and made white, and tried; but the wicked shall do wickedly: and none of the wicked shall understand; but the wise shall understand." Let's focus for a moment on the first part of that verse: "Many shall be purified, and made white, and tried;" Further clarification can be found in Daniel 11:35 and Zechariah 13:9.

Daniel 11:35 reads, "And some of them of understanding shall fall. to try them, and to purge, and to make them white, even to the time of the end: because it is yet for a time appointed." This means some of the saints of understanding will be killed when they try to save people by making them clean. This will occur at the start of the great tribulation when the Antichrist makes war with the saints and the saints are killed, imprisoned, or taken into captivity. This will be the trial of our faith, the saints' faith.

Zechariah 13:9 reads, "And I will bring the third part through the fire, and will refine them as silver is refined, and will try them as gold is tried: they shall call on my name, and I will hear them; I will say, It is my people; and they shall say, The LORD is my God." This passage shows that God will try us as gold is tried during the great tribulation. At that time, two-thirds of the saints will die, and one-third shall be left in all the land of the world. The saints that remain in the land will be tried as gold Zechariah 13:8, it reads, "And it shall come to pass, that in all the land, saith the LORD, two parts therein shall be cut off and die; but the third shall be left therein." The remaining third of the saints will remain and live during the great tribulation. They will still be living when Jesus Christ comes back.

Now let's go back to Daniel 12:10 where it says, "but the wicked shall do wickedly: and none of the wicked shall understand;" We will turn to the books of Hosea and Revelation to discern further meaning. First, Hosea 14:9 reads, "Who is wise, and he shall understand these things? prudent, and he shall know them? for the ways of the LORD are right, and the just shall walk in them: but the transgressors shall fall therein." This verse means the persons who are wise will understand the prophecies of the end time, but the wicked will not.

Revelation 9:20 reads, "And the rest of the men which were not killed by these plagues yet repented not of the works of their hands, that they should not worship devils, and idols of gold, and silver, and brass, and stone, and of wood: which neither can see, nor hear, nor walk:". The rest of the men that are not killed by the plagues do not repent because they are wicked and do not understand. But, the wise will understand.

Revelation 22:11 reads, "He that is unjust, let him be unjust still: and he which is filthy, let him be filthy still: and he that is righteous, let him be righteous still: and he that is holy, let him be holy still." All this will occur during the time of the great tribulation. He that is filthy will remain filthy. He will not understand. He that is righteous will remain righteous. The righteous will understand.

We return once again to Daniel 12:10, this time to where it says, "the wise shall understand." Additional references to this concept occur in the books of Daniel and John. Daniel 11:33 reads, "And they that understand among the people shall instruct many: yet they shall fall by the sword, and by flame, by captivity, and by spoil, many days." The wise will understand and instruct many, but some will be killed, some will be captured, and some will be imprisoned.

Daniel 11:35 also mentions that some of the wise will be killed. It reads, "And some of them of understanding shall fall. to try them, and to purge, and to make them white, even to the time of the end: because it is yet for a time appointed."

John 7:17 relates the words of Jesus: "If any man will do his will, he shall know of the doctrine, whether it be of God, or whether I speak of myself." This means that if any man carries out the will of Jesus, he will know of the doctrine. They will know if Jesus is speaking of God's word or speaking of himself. That is why the Bible says the wise will understand.

John 8:47 then reads, "He that is of God heareth God's words: ye therefore hear them not, because ye are not of God." He that is of God will understand, and they will know if someone is speaking God's words. But if someone is not of God, they will not recognize God's words.

John 18:37 reads, "Pilate therefore said unto him, Art thou a king then? Jesus answered, Thou sayest that I am a king. To this end was I born, and for this cause came I into the world, that I should bear witness unto the truth. Every one that is of the truth, heareth my voice." Everyone that is of the truth hears Jesus. They hear God's words because the wise understand.

Lastly, the final verse of Daniel 12 we will address in this section reads, "And from the time that the daily sacrifice shall be taken away, and the abomination that maketh desolate set up, there shall be a thousand two hundred and ninety days." (Dan. 12:11). Many of the preachers, teachers, and prophets of today teach false doctrine. They talk about when the Jews go back to making animals sacrifice, saying that will make the abomination that maketh desolate, but that is not true. They say the Antichrist will stop the sacrifice and set himself up as God in the temple. Some of them say that will make the abomination that maketh desolate, but that is not what the Bible says.

The Bible says, "And from the time that the daily sacrifice shall be taken away, and the abomination that maketh desolate set up,". (Dan 12:11). The daily sacrifice is the saints of God, and the Antichrist will take it away by making war with the saints, which means he will kill some and imprison some. After he takes away the daily sacrifice, he will set up an image, which will cause the abomination that maketh desolate, just like Nebuchadnezzar did. History repeats itself.

Further reading about the Antichrist's creation of the image can be found in Revelation 13:14. He will make an image to the beast, and he will want all people, nations, and languages to worship it. If they refuse to worship the image of the beast, they should be killed. The image will make the abomination that maketh desolate. God is dealing with the whole world—all nations, including the land of Israel.

Remember when the church first started in the New Testament after the day of the Pentecost. Saul persecuted the church. In doing so, Saul took away the daily sacrifice. Some people were killed and some were imprisoned.

Acts 8:3 tells more of Saul. It reads, "As for Saul, he made havoc of the church, entering into every house, and haling men and women, committed them to prison." This shows further that Saul was taking away the daily sacrifice. Because Daniel's prophecy was for the future, in the New Testament, the daily sacrifice is the saints of God.

REVELATION 13

Now I am going to teach in Revelation 13, starting with verse 1. It reads, "And I stood upon the sand of the sea, and saw a beast rise up out of the sea, having seven heads and ten horns, and upon his horns ten crowns, and upon his heads the name of blasphemy." In his vision, John saw a beast rise from the sea. The beast is one. They are combined and upon the earth now. The lion, the bear, the leopard, and the fourth beast will come up later, but the antichrist is among them.

Revelation 13:1 corresponds with Daniel 7:2–3. "Daniel spake and said, I saw in my vision by night, and behold, the four winds of the heaven strove upon the great sea." (Dan. 7.2). Daniel 7:3 then reads, "And four great beasts came up from the sea, diverse one from another." so,"four great beasts came up from the sea." The sea also means people, so the beasts came from the people. Four great beasts came upon the whole earth.

Then, the portion of Revelation 13:1 that says, "having seven heads and ten horns," corresponds with Revelation 12:3, 17:3, 17:9, and 17:12. Keep in mind that the ten horns are ten kings. The horns represent power.

Revelation 12:3 reads, "And there appeared another wonder in heaven: and behold, a great red dragon, having seven heads and ten horns, and seven crowns upon his heads." You see, John saw this in heaven, but it will also happen here upon the earth. God was simply showing this to John in heaven, but it will happen here on Earth in the end time.

Now let's read Revelation 17:3, 17:9, and 17:12. Verse 3 reads, "So he carried me away in the spirit into the wilderness: and I saw a woman sit upon a scarlet-colored beast, full of names of blasphemy, having seven heads and ten horns." The woman sitting upon the scarlet-colored beast is the Catholic church, the red dragon. The red dragon gave the world government his power, his seat, and great authority. You see, the woman is also the church. This particular church is the apostate church, false churches that teach false doctrine which we see now in America and around the world. False doctrine is everywhere. The false church, which consists of the Vatican—who is also known as the false prophet—will tell the ten horns what to do, and they will control the world.

Revelation 17:9 reads, "And here is the mind which hath wisdom. The seven heads are seven mountains, on which the woman sitteth." The Roman Catholic Church sits on all seven continents; and Rome sits on seven hills, and it could be the seven hills in Israel.

Next, Revelation 17:12 reads, "And the ten horns which thou sawest are ten kings, which have received no kingdom as yet; but receive power as kings one hour with the beast." The ten horns are the ten kings. So, the ten kings will receive power from the beast, the false prophet.

Now we will continue the lesson with Revelation 13:2. It reads, "And the beast which I saw was like unto a leopard, and his feet were as the feet of a bear, and his mouth as the mouth of a lion: and the dragon gave him his power, and his seat, and great authority." These are the same beasts that are in Daniel 7. The first beast is Britain and the United States: the symbol of Britain is the lion, and the symbol of the United States is an eagle. Some of the preachers and teachers say that the symbol of Germany is the leopard. The symbol of the bear is Russia. The mouth of the lion is Britain and the United States because the United States came from Britain.

Now focus on the portion of Revelation 13:2 that reads, "And the beast which I saw was like unto a leopard." From here we will go to Daniel 7:6, which reads, "After this, I beheld, and lo, another, like a leopard, which had upon the back of it four wings of a fowl: the beast had also four heads; and dominion was given to it." The beast government had four heads. It was a combination of the lion, and China, the bear, and the fourth beast, which is also known as the false prophet. After the first three heads are plucked up by the roots, the fourth beast will take over. The fourth beast will exercise all the power of the first beast, the mouth of the lion, and China, and the bear. In Revelation, the Bible shows and tells you a beast will rise out of the sea. The beasts are combined in Revelation, but they are different from one another in Daniel. In Daniel, three of the first beasts shall be plucked up by the roots and the fourth beast shall take over. The fourth beast in Daniel is the same as the second beast is in Revelation 13:11, and both are the Antichrist, the false prophet.

Now let's go back to Revelation 13:2 where it says, "and his feet were as the feet of a bear." As I mentioned previously, the bear stands for Russia. The bear is also referenced in Daniel 7:5. It reads "And behold another beast, a second, like to a bear, and it raised up itself on one side, and it had three ribs in the mouth of it between the teeth of it; and they said thus unto it, Arise,

devour much flesh." Now they will tell the bear to devour much flesh, which means they will tell the bear to kill a lot of people.

Many of the false prophets of today say this has already happened, but that is not true. They claim it happened when Stalin was president of the Soviet Union. After World War II, Stalin killed a lot of people, and the false prophets say that he devoured much flesh. However, what the Bible tells of in Daniel 7:5 hasn't happened yet. The present-day false prophets continue to lie to people, including the one from South Carolina. He also says the devouring of much flesh has already happened, but again, that is not the truth. His taped recording is proof of the lies being told to the people.

Let's now return to Revelation 13:2 where it says, "and his mouth as the mouth of a lion:". This verse corresponds with Daniel 7:4, which reads, "The first was like a lion, and had eagle's wings; I beheld till the wings thereof were plucked, and it was lifted up from the earth, and made stand upon the feet as a man, and a man's heart was given to it." Remember, the lion is Britain, and the eagle's wings represent the United States. "The wings therefore were plucked" (Dan. 7:4) probably means the United States will come down in the new world order. A man's heart was given to it, but it will no longer have a heart after God. Prayer has been taken out schools, and the Ten Commandments and the Bible were taken out of court houses. They don't want anything to do with God. The only things they talk about are human rights, women's rights, children's rights, and abortion. They put women above men. The world is filled with violence because of the love of money. There is no more justice and righteousness in the land. The Lord Jesus Christ is coming back soon. He is the just one, and he will soon return.

Returning to Revelation 13:2 where it says, "the dragon gave him his power," we will reference Revelation 12:9 to gain further insight. It reads, "And the great dragon was cast out, that old serpent, called the Devil, and Satan, which deceiveth the whole world: he was cast out into the earth, and his angels were cast out with him." The Devil gave the beast government his power. That is why the government doesn't have a heart after the heart of God. They serve Satan.

Next, let's go back to once more to Revelation 13:2 where it says, "and his seat," This phrase corresponds with Revelation 16:10, which reads, "And the fifth angel poured out his vial upon the seat of the beast; and his kingdom was full of darkness; and they gnawed their tongues for pain,". The beast's kingdom, consisting of those bearing the mark of the beast, was in pain. This concept sounds similar to a computer chip I have heard about; it will make sores in you if it breaks inside of your body. We are presently watching the first beast, or the first king, that's written about in Daniel 8:21. Bush was the first king in that first beast. It might be soon before the United States horn be broken or plucked up by the roots.

Let us return for a moment to Revelation 12:4, which reads, "And his tail drew the third part of the stars of heaven, and did cast them to the earth: and the dragon stood before the woman which was ready to be delivered, for to devour her child as soon as it was born." The tail stands for the false prophet, the Antichrist. The dragon gave him great authority. The false prophet will deceive many people. On Earth, Satan and his fallen angels get into people and cause them to do evil. The people are captured by the will of Satan.

Satan will also get into the man of sin, the false prophet. God is tired of people, including church people, doing all sorts of sinful things like lying, stealing, killing, and committing adultery and fornication. Men are lying with mankind as they do with women. This is an abomination in the eyes of God. The world is filled with so much violence. God is tired of his people living in sin.

Now, continuing on with the lesson, Revelation 13:3 reads, "And I saw one of his heads as it were wounded to death; and his deadly wound was healed: and all the world wondered after the beast." Most of the present-day false prophets say the wounded head is Germany, who was wounded in World War II and then healed when the Berlin Wall came down in 1989, rejoining East and West Germany. But as I said before, I believe one of the leaders of China the bear, or the lion will get sick or shot unto death, but he will live and recover, and the Antichrist will suggest the creation of an image of the beast whose head was wounded.

Taking a closer look at the meaning of the phrase, "as it were wounded to death; and his deadly wound was healed:" (Rev. 13:3), we turn now to Revelation 13:12 and 13:14 for further clarification. Revelation 13:12 reads, "And he exerciseth all the power of the first beast before him, and causeth the earth and them which dwell therein to worship the first beast, whose deadly wound was healed." This verse likely means the antichrist will exercise all the power of the first beast, the four heads beast China the bear, and the lion, and an image will be made of the head that was wounded.

Revelation 13:14 then reads, "And deceiveth them that dwell on the earth by the means of those miracles which he had power to do in the sight of the beast; saying to them that dwell on the earth, that they should make an image to the beast, which had the wound by the sword, and did live." The false prophet said people should make an image to the beast whose head was wounded by the sword.

Now we will return to Revelation 13:3 where it says, "all the world wondered after the beast." It phrase corresponds with Revelation 17:8, which reads, "The beast that thou sawest, was, and is not; and shall ascend out of the bottomless pit, and go into perdition: and they that dwell on the earth shall wonder, (whose names were not written in the book of life from the foundation of the world,) when they behold the beast that was, and is not, and yet is." The people who dwell on the earth will wonder because only a few will be saved, only the very elect. Only the people that keep God's commandments will be saved.

Revelation then 13:4 reads, "And they worshipped the dragon which gave power unto the beast: and they worshipped the beast, saying, Who is like unto the beast? who is able to make war with him?" Most of the people in the world today are worshipping the dragon and the beast. The dragon is Satan, and the beast is the government that rules other nations, kills people, and makes war with nations that don't do what the government says. We are coming to a one-world government.

Let's look more closely at the phrase, "Who is like unto the beast? who is able to make war with him?" (Revelation 13:4). We can learn more by reading Revelation 18:18: "And cried, when they saw the smoke of her burning, saying, What city is like unto this great city!" I believe the city in this verse is the city that will be moved to Israel, the tabernacles which is the headquarters of the Vatican. There you see the city clothed in fine linen of purple and scarlet and decked with gold, precious stones, and pearls. The cardinals and priests, or Bishop dress in purple and scarlet colors, and the church is decked with gold, precious stones, and pearls.

Next, Revelation 13:5 reads, "And there was given unto him a mouth speaking great things and blasphemies; and power was given unto him to continue forty and two months." The beast government will speak great things, and power will be given unto him to continue for forty and two months. Now, looking back to the first beast in Revelation 13:1–2, John saw one of its heads get wounded to death. After the beast's head was wounded, he continued forty and two months more after the deadly wound was healed. Some people think the verse in Revelation 13:5 talks about the Antichrist, the man of sin, but it is talking about the first beast in Revelation 13:1–2. The Antichrist will also continue forty and two months, but only after he sets up the image of the beast that was wounded.

Now, focusing on where Revelation 13:5 says, "a mouth speaking great things and blasphemies;" we see that it is saying the first and second beasts will speak great things. The book of Daniel can offer further evidence of this. For example, Daniel 7:8 reads, "I considered the horns, and behold there came up among them another little horn, before whom there were three of the first horns plucked up by the roots: and behold, in this horn were eyes like the eyes of man, and a mouth speaking great things." This verse refers to the fourth beast in Daniel and the second beast in Revelation 13:11. The fourth beast will pluck up the first three beasts, which are the lion, the bear, and China. The fourth beast had ten horns and power was given to the ten kings in Revelation 17:12, which reads, "And the ten horns which thou sawest are ten kings, which have received no kingdom as yet; but receive power as kings one hour with the beast." The false prophet, the Antichrist, is the man of sin. He spoke of great things. This is the first and second beast in the book of Revelation.

Daniel 7:11 provides additional insight: "I beheld then because of the voice of the great words which the horn spake: I beheld even till the beast was slain, and his body destroyed, and given to the burning flame." Where the Bible says, "because of the voice of the great words which the horn spake:" it refers to the words of the Antichrist, the man of sin, the false prophet. He spoke these great words, and the beast system will be destroyed.

Daniel 7:25 then reads, "And he shall speak great words against the most High, and shall wear out the saints of the most High, and think to change times and laws: and they shall be given into his hand until a time and times and the dividing of time." The Antichrist will speak great words against the most High—God. He will speak against God thinking he will change time and laws. This is starting to happen now. They are changing laws. Most people, such as pastors, preachers, teachers, and prophets, don't know the laws of God, so they change them. As a result, people worship the beast unknowingly. The teachers, preachers, and the prophets are worshipping the beast.

Daniel 11:36 reads, "And the king shall do according to his will; and he shall exalt himself, and magnify himself above every god, and shall speak marvelous things against the God of gods, and shall prosper till the indignation be accomplished: for that that is determined shall be done." The Antichrist will speak marvelous things against God, the almighty God. He will speak against God and think himself to be God, but he is just a man. He will not be God, not ever. Only the true and living God lasts forever. Thank you, Jesus, the true and living God.

Now let's return to Revelation 13:5 where it says, "forty and two months." For more information, we will turn to Revelation 11:2 and 12:6.

Revelation 11:2 reads, "But the court which is without the temple, leave out, and measure it not; for it is given unto the Gentiles: and the holy city shall they tread under foot forty and two months." The holy city is Jerusalem. This verse says Jerusalem will be taken over by the Gentiles for forty and two months, which is three and a half years. People in Judea will flee to the mountains for three and a half years. That is when the Antichrist will set up that image that will make the abomination that maketh desolate. This will be the start of the great tribulation. But before he sets up the image, he will kill the two witnesses. After he kills the two witnesses, he will set up the image, and Jerusalem will go into captivity for three and a half years. During that time, some of the saints will be killed and some will go into captivity into all nations.

Now let's turn to Luke 21:24. It reads, "And they shall fall by the edge of the sword, and shall be led away captive into all nations: and Jerusalem shall be trodden down of the Gentiles, until the times of the Gentiles be fulfilled." This further illustrates Jerusalem will be trodden down by the Gentiles and go into captivity for three and a half years. Some shall be killed, and the church will have to flee from the serpent (the devil) and into the wilderness.

Revelation 12:6 reads, "And the woman fled into the wilderness, where she hath a place prepared of God, that they should feed her there a thousand two hundred and threescore days." In this passage, the woman is the church, the saints. It says she will have to flee into the wilderness for three and a half years, which is the same as forty and two months.

Now let's continue to Revelation 13:6. It reads, "And he opened his mouth in blasphemy against God, to blaspheme his name, and his tabernacle, and them that dwell in heaven." Focusing on the phrase, "and his tabernacle, and them that dwell in heaven," we turn to the books of John and Colossians for further explanation.

John 1:14 reads, "And the word was made flesh, and dwelt among us, (and we beheld his glory, the glory as of the only begotten of the Father,) full of grace and truth." The phrase "the word was made flesh" means the beast, the government leader, will blaspheme God and his tabernacle. The tabernacle is the body of Christ. Colossians 2:9 reads, "For in him dwelleth all the fullness of the Godhead bodily." God was in Jesus Christ, and the beast government leader will blaspheme God.

Let's continue in Revelation 13:7, which reads, "And it was given unto him to make war with the saints, and to overcome them: and power was given him over all kindreds, and tongues, and nations." You see, the power was given unto that third beast to make war with the saints, not animals. This is further proof that the daily sacrifice is not animal sacrifice, but rather it is the saints of God.

Now focusing on where it says, "to make war with the saints, and to overcome them:" (Rev. 13:7), we look to Daniel 7:21 and Revelation 11:7 and 12:17 for additional information. The false prophets of today say the Antichrist will take away animal sacrifice. While he will stop the animal sacrifice, the Bible is talking about the daily sacrifice. It talks about taking away the saints of God, putting some of them in prison and killing some. The Antichrist will make war with the saints.

Daniel 7:21 reads, "I beheld, and the same horn made war with the saints, and prevailed against them;" The horn referenced in this verse stands for the Antichrist, the false prophet, the man of sin, who is the second beast in Revelation and the fourth beast in Daniel. Next we turn to Revelation 11:7, which reads, "And when they shall have finished their testimony, the beast that ascendeth out of the bottomless pit shall make war against them, and shall overcome them, and kill them." The beast will make war with the saints, and he will kill the two witnesses. That is when the great tribulation will start, which means there shall be great tribulation, great persecution, for the saints. It will last for three and a half years.

Revelation 12:17 then reads, "And the dragon was wroth with the woman, and went to make war with the remnant of her seed, which keep the commandments of God, and have the testimony of Jesus Christ." In this verse, the dragon is Satan, and the woman is the church, the saints. Satan was angry with the saints. He will make war with them because they keep the commandments of God and have the testimony of Jesus Christ.

I am trying to get the people of God to understand the Bible's prophecy. The people today's churches are angry with the saints of God. Churches are polluted. There are things in the churches such as adultery, fornication, homosexuality, and women preachers. God is not in the churches. He has left them. These people claim they are Christians, but they are not.

Next, let's divide Revelation 13:7 where it says, "and power was given him over all kindreds and tongues and nations." For further clarification, we turn to Revelation 11:18 and Revelation 17:15. Revelation 11:18 reads, "And the nations were angry, and thy wrath is come, and the time of the dead, that they should be judged, and that thou shouldest give reward unto thy servants the prophets, and to the saints, and them that fear thy name, small and great; and shouldest destroy them which destroy the earth." The power over all nations was given to the beast government, but when the Lord comes back, the nations will be angry because God will come and destroy the wicked. The people will not be able to do the things they did before.

Revelation 17:15 then reads, "And he saith unto me, 'The waters which thou sawest, where the whore sitteth, are peoples, and multitudes, and nations, and tongues." This means the beast government will control all peoples, and multitudes, and nations, and tongues. This beast government is the Antichrist, the man of sin.

Let's continue in Revelation 13:8, which reads, "And all that dwell upon the earth shall worship him, whose names are not written in the book of life of the Lamb slain from the foundation of the world." Let's look more closely at where it says, "whose names are not written in the book of life of the Lamb slain". To do so, we will turn to Exodus 32:32; Daniel 12:1; Philippians 4:3; Revelation 3:5, 20:12 and 21:27.

Exodus 32:32 reads, "Yet now, if thou wilt forgive their sin: and if not, blot me, I pray thee, out of thy book which thou hast written." You see Moses wanted the Lord to blot his name out of the book of life. "And the LORD said unto Moses, Whosoever hath sinned against me, him will I blot out of my book." (Exod. 32:33) You see the word "book" with no s is for the righteous—the saints. The word "books" with the letter s is for the wicked—the sinners.

Daniel 12:1 reads, "And at that time shall Michael stand up, the great prince which standeth for the children of thy people: and there shall be a time of trouble, such as never was since there was a nation even to that same time: and at that time thy people shall be delivered, every one that shall be found written in the book." There is no s on the word "book," so the book is for the righteous in this verse.

Philippians 4:3 reads, "And I entreat thee also, true yoke-fellow, help those women which labored with me in the gospel, with Clement also, and with other my fellow laborers, whose names are in the book of life." The book of life is a single book, with no s.

Revelation 3:5 reads, "He that overcometh, the same shall be clothed in white raiment; and I will not blot out his name out of the book of life, but I will confess his name before my Father, and before his angels." Your name must be written in the book of life and not blotted out.

Revelation 20:12 reads, "And I saw the dead, small and great, stand before God; and the books were opened: and another book was opened, which is the book of life: and the dead were judged out of those things which were written in the books, according to their works." The unrighteous were judged out of the things that were written in the books. Notice there is an s—books.

Revelation 21:27 reads, "And there shall in no wise enter into it any thing that defileth, neither whatsoever worketh abomination, or maketh a lie; but they which are written in the Lamb's book of life." In order to be written in the Lamb's book of life, you have to stop sinning and repent. You have to get baptized in the name of the Lord Jesus Christ.

Now let's go back to Revelation 13:8 where it says, "from the foundation of the world." From here we go to Revelation 17:8, which reads, "The beast that thou sawest, was, and is not; and shall ascend out of the bottomless pit, and go into perdition: and they that dwell on the earth shall wonder, (whose names were not written in the book of life from the foundation of the world,) when they behold the beast that was, and is not, and yet is." The saints' names are written in the book of life, and the Antichrist will make war with the saints. Those that dwell on the earth will wonder whose names were not written in the book of life because almost everyone on the earth will have worshipped the Antichrist except the saints.

Let's continue on and read Revelation 13:9. It says, "If any man have an ear, let him hear." From here, we will look to Revelation 2:7 for further clarification. It reads, "He that hath an ear, let him hear what the Spirit saith unto the churches; To him that overcometh will I give to eat of the tree of life, which is in the midst of the paradise of God."

Let's continue in Revelation 13:10, which reads, "He that leadeth into captivity, shall go into captivity: he that killeth with the sword, must be killed with the sword. Here is the patience and the faith of the saints." If we focus on where it says, ""He that leadeth into captivity, shall go into captivity:" we can turn to Isaiah 33:1, which reads, "Wo to thee that spoilest, and thou wast not spoiled; and dealest treacherously, and they dealt not treacherously with thee! When thou shalt cease to spoil, thou shalt be spoiled; and when thou shalt make an end to deal treacherously, they shall deal treacherously with thee." These passages warn sinners to stop doing bad things like stealing. They will come back and get you for your sins, no matter if you committed them fifty years ago. They will not forgive you, even if you stop sinning. That is exactly how it is now: there is no forgiveness. They will deal with you treacherously (Isa. 33:1) means they will be untrustworthy. They will be unmerciful unto you and will have no forgiveness.

Now back to Revelation 13:10 where it says, "he that killeth with the sword must be killed." It goes to the books of Genesis and Matthew. Genesis 9:6 reads, "Whoso sheddeth man's blood, by man shall his blood be shed: for in the image of God made he man." This means if you killed someone, you will be put to death. Matthew 26:52 reads, "Then said Jesus unto him, Put up again thy sword into his place: for all they that take the sword, shall perish with the sword." They that take the sword will die by the sword, which simply means all who have killed shall be killed.

Returning to Revelation 13:10 where it says, "Here is the patience and the faith of the saints," we then look to Revelation 14:12. Revelation 14:12 reads, "Here is the patience of the saints: here are they that keep the commandments of God, and the faith of Jesus." The saints are supposed to have patience because there is another beast coming up after this first beast.

Let's continue on to Revelation 13:11. It reads, "And I beheld another beast coming up out of the earth, and he had two horns like a lamb, and he spake as a dragon." A beast is a king that rules other nations. The fact that this beast has two horns means he has two sources of power: government and religious power. It is just like Nebuchadnezzar. He controlled government and religion. Whomever he wanted killed, he killed, and the ones that didn't bow down to the image he had set up would be cast into the midst of a burning fiery furnace. At the end time, the king will do the same thing. The king is the Antichrist, the false prophet.

Back to Revelation 13:11, let's focus on where it says, "coming up out of the earth, and he had two horns like a lamb, and he spake as a dragon." It goes to Revelation 11:7, which reads, "And when they shall have finished their testimony, the beast that ascendeth out of the bottomless pit shall make war against them, and shall overcome them, and kill them." Now you see, this refers to the second beast in Revelation 13:11 that kill the two witnesses.

The second beast is the false prophet. He exercised all the power of the first beast before him. The beast that was before him was the leopard, the bear, and the mouth of the lion. He controlled governments in the world. Today, the lion and the eagle are the first beast. We still in the first and second feast two more to go through before it is all over.

Now let's continue in Revelation 13:12, which reads, "And he exerciseth all the power of the first beast before him, and causeth the earth and them which dwell therein to worship the first beast, whose deadly wound was healed." The false prophet will cause the people to worship the first beast, whose deadly wound was healed. One of the heads of the first beast was: either the lion, the bear, or the leopard.

Let's rightly divide the word of truth where it says, "whose deadly wound was healed." We turn to Revelation 13:3 for clarification. It reads, "And I saw one of his heads as it were wounded to death; and his deadly wound was healed: and all the world wondered after the beast." This shows that one of the beast's heads will get wounded unto death.

Let's continue in Revelation 13:13. It reads, "And he doeth great wonders, so that he maketh fire come down from heaven on the earth in the sight of men." He will do great wonders, but he is the false prophet. People will worship the beast, all except the very elect.

Now, rightly dividing the word of truth where it says, "he doeth great wonders," we go to the books of Deuteronomy 13:1–3, Matthew 24:24, 2 Thessalonians 2:9, and Revelation 16:14. Deuteronomy 13:1 reads, "If there arise among you a prophet, or a dreamer of dreams, and giveth thee a sign or a wonders," The false prophets of today will show signs and lying wonders. They are showing signs now. One of them says, "I am the sign."

Deuteronomy 13:2 reads, "And the sign or the wonder come to pass, whereof he spake unto thee, saying, Let us go after other gods, which thou hast not known, and let us serve them;" When the prophets of today speak in the name of the Lord and their vision does not follow or come to pass, the Lord did not speak and the prophet is false. And the false prophets will say to the Lord, "Have we not prophesied in thy name? And in thy name have cast out devils? And in thy name done many wonderful works?"

Next, Deuteronomy 13:3 reads, "Thou shalt not hearken unto the words of that prophet, or that dreamer of dreams: for the LORD your God proveth you, to know whether ye love the LORD your God with all your heart and with all your soul." You see, the Lord will prove you and whether you love him with all of your heart, soul, mind, and strength. You will not follow that false prophet or hearken unto that false prophet.

Matthew 24:24 reads, "For there shall arise false Christs, and false prophets, and shall show great signs and wonders; insomuch that, if it were possible, they shall deceive the very elect." The elect will come to the Lord Jesus Christ. Jesus said, "All that the Father giveth me, shall come to me; and him that cometh to me I will in no wise cast out" (John 6:37). You see, "The foundation of God standeth sure, having this seal, The Lord knoweth them that are his." (2 Tim. 2:19). So God's elect won't be deceived.

Second Thessalonians 2:9 reads, "Even him, whose coming is after the working of Satan, with all power, and signs, and lying wonders,". This passage shows that Jesus Christ will come after the working of Satan. During the great tribulation, Satan will be doing his work—making war with the saints. During the great tribulation, the Antichrist will come "with all power, and signs, and lying wonders." Jesus will come immediately after the tribulation of those days.

Revelation 16:14 reads, "For they are the spirits of devils, working miracles, which go forth unto the kings of the earth, and of the whole world, to gather them to the battle of that great day of God Almighty." This verse shows that the Antichrist will be doing miracles and deceiving the people on the earth. They will be fooled by these miracles.

Now let's go back to Revelation 13:13 where it says, "so that he maketh fire come down from heaven on the earth in the sight of men." Additional details regarding this verse can be found in the books of 1 Kings and 2 Kings. First Kings 18:38 reads, "Then the fire of the LORD fell, and consumed the burnt sacrifice, and the wood, and the stones, and the dust, and licked up the water that was in the trench." In this verse, Elijah called fire from the heaven. The Antichrist will also call fire from the heaven, "in the sight of men" (Rev. 13:13).

Next, 2 Kings 1:10 reads, "And Elijah answered and said to the captain of fifty, If I be a man of God, then let fire come down from heaven, and consume thee and thy fifty. And there came down fire from heaven, and consumed him and his fifty." You see, Elijah said "let fire come down," and fire came down from heaven. Second Kings 1:12 then reads, "And Elijah answered and said unto them, If I be a man of God, let fire come down from heaven, and consume thee and thy fifty. And the fire of God came down from heaven, and consumed him and his fifty." The Antichrist, too, will call fire down from heaven in the sight of men and thereby deceive the people.

Now Revelation 13:14 reads, "And deceiveth them that dwell on the earth by the means of those miracles which he had power to do in the sight of the beast; saying to them that dwell on the earth, that they should make an image to the beast, which had the wound by the sword, and did live." The false prophet, the Antichrist, will tell the people they should make an image to the beast that was wounded and lived. The image will be a statue or a robot

Now let's look a little closer at where it says, "deceiveth them that dwell on the earth" We will find further evidence in Revelation 12:9 and Revelation 19:20. Revelation 12:9 reads, "And the great dragon was cast out, that old serpent, called the Devil, and Satan, which deceiveth the whole world: he was cast out into the earth, and his angels were cast out with him." Satan will be in that false prophet, the Antichrist. He will be the false prophet that will deceive the people. He will want them to receive the mark of the beast and worship his image.

Now Revelation 19:20 reads, "And the beast was taken, and with him the false prophet that wrought miracles before him, with which he deceived them that had received the mark of the beast, and them that worshiped his image. These both were cast alive into a lake of fire burning with brimstone." The false prophet deceived the people to receive the mark of the beast and worship the beast's image. "And that no man might buy or sell, save he that had the mark, or the name of the beast, or the number of his name" (Rev. 13:17).

Let's now look more closely at the verse in Revelation 13:14 where it says, "by the means of those miracles which he had power to do in the sight of the beast;". To gain further insight, we turn to 2 Thessalonians 2:9, which reads, "Even him, whose coming is after the working of Satan, with all power, and signs, and lying wonders,". This verse speaks of who will come after the working of Satan: Jesus

Christ. Satan will work hard during the great tribulation, and Jesus will come immediately after the tribulation of those days.

Satan will work "with all power, and signs, and lying wonders," like all of the lying preachers, teachers, and prophets of today. They will say that they are telling the truth. So why then, within the next month, six months, or year, will they change their words or say something different about the verses in the Bible? They keep claiming they tell the truth about the verses in the Bible, but within the next six months or year, they will change.

God's word does not change. The truth does not change. These preachers, teachers, and prophets have not been telling the truth. For example, the false prophet from South Carolina, R. G. Stair, tells the people, "I am telling you the truth. I lie not." But within the next six months to a year, he will say something different. He says different things about the same verse, but he claims he lies not. The truth does not change.

The first thing Jesus told his disciples is to take heed that no man deceive them. Jesus said there will be false Christs. He was also speaking to the saints who will be here at the end time. He wanted them to take heed that no man deceive them. He said many false prophets shall arise and deceive many. The false prophet from South Carolina thinks himself to be above that which is written in the Bible. He loves the praise of men, and he calls himself the son of man.

Let's look a little more closely at Revelation 13:14 where it says, "and did live." For this we will turn to 2 Kings 20:7. It reads, "And Isaiah said, Take a lump of figs. And they took and laid it on the boil, and he recovered." This is a reflection of the beast head that was wounded by the sword, and he recovered. He was either shot or sick unto death, but he recovered from it.

Next, Revelation 13:15 goes on to read, "And he had power to give life unto the image of the beast, that the image of the beast should both speak, and cause that as many as would not worship the image of the beast should be killed." The Antichrist had power to give life unto the image of the beast that was wounded but lived, the statue the people made unto the beast. The statue should speak, and the head that was wounded shall live.

Now let's consider where verse 15 says, "and cause that as many as would not worship the image of the beast should be killed." If you don't want to worship the image of the beast that the Antichrist sets up, you should be killed. It is just like what Nebuchadnezzar did. He set up an image, and he wanted everyone to worship it. All who did not worship the image thrown in the fire, and killed. Many people will worship the beast's image and receive the mark of the beast. The false prophets, preachers, and teachers of today say the saints won't be here during the great tribulation. That is not the truth. The saints that are still living will be here.

Now let's go back to where Revelation 13:15 says, "and cause that as many as would not worship the image of the beast should be killed." It goes to Revelation 16:2, which reads, "And the first went, and poured out his vial upon the earth; and there fell a noisome and grievous sore upon the men which had the mark of the beast, and upon them which worshipped his image."

If you take the mark of the beast, you will receive a noisome and grievous sore upon you, as will all who worshiped the image. People do not understand, and they do not want to hear. Their ears are dull of hearing. Many will receive the mark of the beast and worship his image.

Revelation 19:20 reads, "And the beast was taken, and with him the false prophet that wrought miracles before him, with which he deceived them that had received the mark of the beast, and them that worshipped his image. These both were cast alive into a lake of fire burning with brimstone." The false prophet, the Antichrist, deceived many people and they received the mark of the beast. I believe the mark of the beast is a computer chip injected under the skin in your right hand or in your forehead.

Revelation 20:4 reads, "And I saw thrones, and they sat upon them, and judgment was given unto them: and I saw the souls of them that were beheaded for the witness of Jesus, and for the word of God, and which had not worshipped the beast, neither his image, neither had received his mark upon their foreheads, or in their hands; and they lived and reigned with Christ a thousand years." The saints that did not worship the beast or his image or received his mark were beheaded for the witness of Jesus, and the word of God, However, they lived and reigned with Jesus for a thousand years.

In Revelation 14:9–11, it says the people that worship the image and receive the mark will be destroyed. Revelation 14:9 reads, "And the third angel followed them, saying with a loud voice, If any man worship the beast and his image, and receive his mark in his forehead, or in his hand,". Next, Revelation 14:10 reads, "The same shall drink of the wine of the wrath of God, which is poured out without mixture into the cup of his indignation; and he shall be tormented with fire and brimstone in the presence of the holy angels, and in the presence of the Lamb:" Lastly, Revelation 14:11 reads, "And the smoke of their torment ascendeth up for ever and ever: and they have no rest day nor night, who worship the beast and his image, and whosoever receiveth the mark of his name." Now take heed. The word of God clearly warns us, if any man worship the beast and his image, and receives his mark in his forehead, or in his hand, they shall be tormented forever.

Returning to Revelation 13:16, it reads "And he causeth all, both small and great, rich and poor, free and bond, to receive a mark in their right hand, or in their foreheads:" The Antichrist will cause all, to receive the mark in their hands, or in their foreheads, but the saints will not receive the mark of the beast.

Now, rightly dividing the word of truth where it says, "to receive a mark in their right hand, or in their foreheads," it takes us to Revelation 14:9, 19:20, and 20:4. Revelation 14:9 reads, "And the third angel followed them, saying with a loud voice, If any man worship the beast and his image, and receive his mark in his forehead, or in his hand," If you receive the mark of the beast or worship the beast and his image, you will be tormented forever with fire and brimstone. The Antichrist won't make you receive the mark, but he will cause you to receive it. For example, if you work for a certain company, they will require you to have a computer chip in your right hand to have access to the building or to open the door. No one will be able to enter the building unless they have the computer chip. I believe the mark of the beast will be a computer chip in your right hand or your forehead. The beast's mark, number, or the number of his name will be used for buying and selling.

Now Revelation 19:20 reads, "And the beast was taken, and with him the false prophet that wrought miracles before him, with which he deceived them that had received the mark of the beast, and them that worshipped his image. These both were cast alive into a lake of fire burning with brimstone." The false prophet deceived people to receive the mark of the beast. The false prophet is the Antichrist, and he deceived people to worship the image of the beast.

Revelation 20:4 reads, "And I saw thrones, and they sat upon them, and judgment was given unto them: and I saw the souls of them that were beheaded for the witness of Jesus, and for the word of God, and which had not worshipped the beast, neither his image, neither had received his mark upon their foreheads, or in their hands, and they lived and reigned with Christ a thousand years." The saints did not receive the mark of the beast in their foreheads. They achieved victory over the image of the beast, his mark, and the number.

Let's continue in Revelation 13:17. It reads, "And that no man might buy or sell, save he that had the mark, or the name of the beast, or the number of his name." This is evidence that people won't be able to buy or sell anything unless they have the mark of the beast, which I believe will be a computer chip in their foreheads or hands. This will be the worst time ever since there was a nation.

Let's look more closely at the phrase, "the name of the beast." Additional insight on this phrase can be found in Revelation 14:11. It reads, "And the smoke of their torment ascendeth up for ever and ever: and they have no rest day nor night, who worship the beast and his image, and whosoever receiveth the mark of his name." This verse again shows that if you receive the mark of the beast, you will be tormented forever and ever, and you will have no rest, day or night. This will be the punishment for whoever worships the beast and his image or whoever receives the mark of his name.

Next, we will study in more detail the portion of Revelation 13:17 that says, "or the number of his name." It goes to Revelation 15:2, which reads, "And I saw as it were a sea of glass mingled with fire: and them that had gotten the victory over the beast, and over his image, and over his mark, and over the number of his name, stand on the sea of glass, having the harps of God." This verse shows that the saints got the victory over the number of the beast's name.

One interpretation of "the number of his name" in today's world is the social security number. The credit card could also be the number of his name because it is also made up of several numbers. You also have to use a pin number in order to buy things. The same thing goes for the welfare or debit card. All of these cards have numbers on them, and you use them to buy things. Bar codes have numbers, and most companies like Wal-Mart have to use bar codes to sell their products. This is how the government keeps track of how much money Wal-Mart takes in each day. Barcodes keep Wal-mart and others from being able to cheat the government in taxes.

Moving on, Revelation 13:18 reads, "Here is wisdom. Let him that hath understanding count the number of the beast: for it is the number of a man; and his number is six hundred threescore and six." Rightly dividing the word of truth where it says, "Here is wisdom," We turn to Revelation 17:9, which reads, "And here is the mind which hath wisdom. The seven heads are seven mountains, on which the woman sitteth." Rome sits on seven hills and seven continents, and the Roman Catholic Church sits around the world. Now the seven hills can be around where the antichrist will rule from Jerusalem.

Let's go back to the phrase, "the number of the beast:" The beast (government) uses numbers to identify you. They use numbers like social security numbers, telephone numbers, microchips on animals, credit cards, driver's licenses, etc. That is why the Bible says, "Let him that hath understanding count the number of the beast:" The time is getting close for Jesus Christ to come back. God is great. He is a great and powerful God. His word is being fulfilled. Thank you, Jesus. Praise the Lord, the everlasting God.

Now let us go back to Revelation 13:18 where it says, "for it is the number of a man; and his number is six hundred threescores and six." That means that a man came up with the number. Taking a closer look at the word of truth where it says, "for it is the number of a man;"

we will turn to Revelation 21:17, which reads, "And he measured the wall thereof, a hundred and forty and four cubits, according to the measure of a man, that is, of the angel." The angel measured the wall of Jerusalem. A hundred and forty and four cubits is the number that came from God. That number did not come from man. Let's figure out the number one hundred and forty and four cubits. A cubit is approximately 18 inches. So, 18 x 144 = 2592 inches. That number came from God.

However, the number 666 came from man. Man also came up with the number to run the computer. I have heard that the computer runs off the number 666 to cover all numbers. Man made that computer, so the number came from man.

Remember when God told Noah to make an ark in Genesis 6:15: "And this is the fashion which thou shalt make it of: The length of the ark shall be three hundred cubits, the breath of it fifty cubits, and the height of it thirty cubits." This number came from God.

The number 666 was made by man for the computer. It did not come from God. Another example is Nebuchadnezzar. He set up an image whose height was threescore cubits, which is 1,080 inches. The breath was six cubits, which 108 inches. The numbers for the image that Nebuchadnezzar made did not come from God because God said in his commandments, "Thou shalt not make unto thee any graven image,"

Leviticus 26:1 says, "Ye shall make you no idols nor graven image, neither rear you up a standing image, neither shall ye set up any image of stone in your land, to bow down unto it: for I am the LORD your God." God said not to rear up a standing image, or put any image of stone on the land. But this is exactly what Nebuchadnezzar did: he set up an image. He wanted everyone to bow down and worship it. This is what the Antichrist will do as well. They will kill the two witnesses, and the Antichrist will take over Jerusalem. He will set up an image and will want everyone to bow down and worship it. Whosoever does not bow down and worship the image should be killed. This happened in the first Babylon. Nebuchadnezzar took over Jerusalem, and Jerusalem went into captivity for seventy years. The Antichrist will take over Jerusalem, and it will go into captivity for three and a half years. Once he sets up an image, all who will not bow down and worship it should be killed.

Now let's go back to the number of the beast, which is the number of a man. Once again, man came up with the number 666 to run a computer. It did not come from God. Some of today's false prophets say that by using the Roman numeral alphabets such as X or L, Ronald Reagan's name came out to be 666. They also say Bill Clinton and Henry Kissinger's names came out to be 666. This shows that people are looking for a man to be named or called 666. However, that is not the case. A man will not be 666. The computer is 666.

The Antichrist will control people by computer. Buying and selling is controlled by numbers. Every product has number that goes into the computer in order for people to buy. People are given social security numbers or telephone numbers to identify them. When they put a computer chip in a person, the numbers on the computer chip will identify that individual person. The computer chip in your hand or in your forehead is the mark of the beast. Like I said before, people will volunteer to receive the beast's mark, the computer chip, in their hands or foreheads. This will allow them to buy or sell. Then when enough people get it, the Antichrist will come in and take over. The man of sin will demand that people have the mark of the beast (also called the computer chip, the name of the beast, or the number of his name) in order to buy or sell.

It is similar to what the insurance people have done. They wanted people to volunteer to have insurance. When enough people got insurance, they made it mandatory for everyone. The Antichrist will do the same thing. He will wait until enough people get the mark of the beast, and then he will pass a law that requires everyone to have it in order to buy or sell.

Now the two witnesses will probably show up just before or around the same time when the ten horns (the ten kings) and the antichrist show up. Most of the so-call Christians believe that now is the time for the two witnesses to show up, but it is not time for the two witnesses because we are not in the third beast yet. We are still in the first and second beast

Revelation 18:10 reads, "Standing afar off for the fear of her torment, saying, Alas, alas! that great city Babylon, that mighty city! For in one hour is thy judgment come." Babylon will be destroyed in one hour. Some of the false prophets say what you read about in Revelation 18 is the United States, but that is not the truth. It is the Vatican, that great city, "which reigneth over the kings of the earth" (Rev. 17:18). The false prophet, who is from the Vatican (the last pope during the fourth beast government), will come in by flatteries, and the ten kings will "receive power as kings one hour with the beast" (Rev. 17:12).

Now the United States is the first beast government on Earth in the last days, which is the beginning of Babylon. The false prophet, along with the ten kings, is the fourth beast in Daniel and the second beast in Revelation. The last beast government will be the end of Babylon, which is destroyed in Revelation 18. The ten kings will destroy the great city of Babylon in one hour. They will "burn her with fire" (Rev. 17:16).

When the United States fights Iran and after that his horn and power will be broken. This means that the U.S. will probably collapse. There will be no more authority in the world, and there will possibly be war here in America caused by the corruption of the people in high offices. The war will even take place in the churches from the prophets on down to the priests. Our justice system in America is corrupt. There isn't any more justice anymore in the land. They say that this is because of the new world order. The new world order is about technology, changing laws, and think to change God's law against men (like human rights, women's rights, and children's rights). They take all the rights away from men. Where are men's rights? You never hear anyone mention anything about men's rights because they took them away. They gave all the rights to women and children. However, we are just in the first beast.

Finally, I would like to say women will rule over us because the word of God says so. In Isaiah 3:12 it says, "As for my people, children are their oppressors, and women rule over them. O my people, they which lead thee cause thee to err. and destroy the way of thy paths."

When women rule over men, then the nations become weak and filled with violence. This is why we are having violence now between women and men and boys and girls. It is because women are ruling over men. This is happening all over the world, and the people are wondering why men are so violent toward women. It is because he is not the head of his wife and children anymore.

They take away all his rights from him. This is why men are getting more violent. The women are getting more violent and angry with men. It is because the women are working and making their own money. No man can tell them anything, and it leads to violence with men and women.

It is now taking its toll. Welcome to the new world order, a world that is filled with violence and corruption. Now people want to know where we are in the Bible prophecy. We are where Jesus Christ talked about in Matthew 24:7. "For nation shall rise against nation, and kingdom against kingdom: and there shall be famines, and pestilences, and earthquakes in divers places." It is because of all the spying on nations and people. And Jesus said "Many false prophets shall rise, and shall deceive many" because a lots of them jump to the end too quick. This is why they are false prophets.

Now we are in the second beast, the Russian bear. He will have three countries in his mouth. This is where we are in the Bible prophecy. The bear will devour much flesh, and he will kill a lot of people.

Like I said before on page eleven, he will rule a certain part of the world. I also said earlier that the United States horn will be broken. Now the second beast is coming in. These four great beasts will overlap each other. Before one gets out, the other one comes in. But the second beast is coming in before the United States' horn is broken. Russia will devour much flesh. It could happen before the United States' horn is broken, or it could happen after the United States' horn is broken because Russia will be part of the third beast.

We are now, in the first, and second beast the United State, and Britain is the first beast. the second beast is Russia, the bear, and the third beast is the leopard, and the leopard will come up, after the U.S. horn is broken.

Then after the third beast. then cometh the fourth beast with the ten horns, ten kings, and the little horn come up among the ten horns, and this is the fourth, and final beast. that you read about in REVELATION: Ch. 17 and Ch. 18

www.ingramcontent.com/pod-product-compliance
Lightning Source LLC
Chambersburg PA
CBHW021128130626
46554CB00002B/917